For me the game couldn't have started better. From the kick-off we worked the ball straight up field and I ran into space for a cross which I met perfectly by stretching out my left foot. Before I realized it the ball was in the back of the net and the goal had come so quickly that even the England fans had been stunned into silence by the speed of it all. It was a peculiar feeling seeing the ball in the net so quickly. For a few seconds the world stopped and fell silent as I turned to celebrate. There was such a look of utter disbelief on the French faces that I had to look back at the goal and then at the referee to make sure I'd scored. The goal was officially timed at twenty-seven seconds. The fastest goal in the history of the World Cup Finals . . .

BRYAN ROBSON
with Tim Russon

# United I Stand

PANTHER
Granada Publishing

Panther Books
Granada Publishing Ltd
8 Grafton Street, London W1X 3LA

This revised edition published by Panther Books 1985

First published in Great Britain by
Pelham Books Ltd 1984



ISBN 0-586-06476-1

Printed and bound in Great Britain by
Collins, Glasgow

Set in Times

# Contents

*Photo credits*
The author and publishers are grateful to Bob Thomas for permission to reproduce copyright photographs.

# 1

## *'Just Bad Luck'*

I could still hear the rumbling roars of the crowd as the ambulance door slammed to. But they were soon drifting away as we hurried through the West Bromwich streets on a journey I sadly knew all too well.

My heart was thundering as the sweat spilled on to the grey woolly stretcher blanket. My leg felt as though it were in an ever tightening vice.

The only thing I was sure of was that for the third time in seven months I had broken my leg.

The journey from the Hawthorns football ground to the district hospital can only be five minutes at most but that sunny April afternoon it felt like fifty.

Just ten minutes had gone of the game against Manchester City when I slid into a tackle and my right leg snapped. Daring to look down I saw a lump swelling up. The pain pulled at my face and players rushed to help from all directions.

From then on it was just a daze. A recurring dream for me of looking up from the field to see worried and anxious faces looking down. The splints were strapped to my leg and the stretcher was hauled up and away. Sympathetic applause from the crowd is no consolation and I knew what they were thinking.

'There goes Robson – we'll be lucky if we ever see him again.'

As I came round in the ambulance there were my mother and girlfriend Denise sitting opposite. Mam had come down from home for the day to watch the game and Denise was there as always to cheer me on.

I could see the looks of anxiety on their faces. They matched those of the team mates I had just left at the ground. They tried to be reassuring but it wasn't going to help. Their words floated above me as a thousand thoughts whirled around my head.

For a young player, football can be a hard and at times desperate life. So many set out on the path to the top and yet so few actually seem to get there. I was supposed to be one of the lucky ones. Here I was, twenty years old and playing my first season in the first division.

I had fought my way up, and this year was to be the one when the name of Bryan Robson was going to spread far beyond the tight world of West Bromwich, or so I thought.

Only a few weeks before I had been selected for the England under-21 squad and after two broken legs everyone was telling me my injury problems were over.

But here I was again, on my way to hospital with the whole future clouded in doubt. My first injury had come back in October. We were playing Spurs at home and I was at left-back. Chris Jones was on to a loose ball and about to shoot when I came sliding in and managed to toe poke the ball away. His boot caught mine and my left leg went numb. I did not really know what to do. I couldn't stand up and our keeper, that colourful character John Osborne was screaming at me to get up and get out.

Nobody ever ignored Ossy, and managing to pull myself up I looked across to the bench where our physio George Wright, was ready to run on. He came on, took a look at my leg, gave it a rub and applied the usual painkilling spray and then told me to play out wide and ease my way back into the game. At first the leg seemed to be on the mend but when the next ball came my way it folded underneath me and I knew then I couldn't go on.

George ran on again to give me a piggyback into the

dressing room and later my leg was strapped up. Both physio and doctor thought it was badly bruised and so did I, it was feeling stronger by the minute.

Denise was there as always to meet me afterwards and a 4-2 win over Spurs was good enough call for celebration, especially when Albion, the first division new boys, were up to third spot in the table.

The after match celebrations, talk of the game, the usual chit chat and round of jokes and wisecracks took my mind off the leg.

A group of us went on for a meal but the dull, nagging ache from the leg was getting worse and when the others decided to go to a local club, I reckoned it was time to call it a day.

That night and all Sunday the leg got more and more painful and when Monday morning came I was at the ground soon after nine hoping that George would come up with some magical cure. He took one look at the swelling and arranged an X-ray at the local hospital.

I remember how my heart sank when the nurse came in and told me it was broken. It was something that had been biting at the back of my thoughts all weekend but I had chosen to convince myself it was just bruised or badly sprained. It was not a bad break though, and they were quick to point that out but it still meant a heavy plaster and a few weeks on the sidelines.

I had fought hard for my place in the team and was just getting settled and now this. At first there was that bitter feeling of disappointment and frustration but I made up my mind I would work and train as never before to get fit again.

Special exercises under the careful supervision of the club's training staff saw me back to fitness in no time at all. I shared my afternoons with George Wright, the club's excellent physio who could be a demanding man but nevertheless a fair one. Gradually the leg was built up. The training had worked better than I dreamed of and after only five weeks I was ready again.

The comeback was fixed, a reserve game against Stoke City at the Hawthorns and a bonus, I was down to play in my favourite midfield role. Get through this one I was told by the player manager Johnny Giles and a first-team place would be there.

But only minutes had gone on that grey, miserable day when I found myself going for a fifty-fifty ball. Some players have trouble with their courage after a break but I never had a thought of it going again. I had always been strong in the tackle and in I went to challenge without giving it a second thought.

As I made contact a sharp breathtaking pain ripped up through me and I was tumbling down. This time there was no need for an X-ray, I knew and so did everybody else that the left leg had gone in exactly the same place.

As the ambulance drew up outside the ground a wave of panic came across me. The world of football was full of men who had been beaten by injury and here I was again on my way to hospital.

A strained fracture was diagnosed and the manager went out of his way to ease my early fears. I liked John Giles, he was of course a great player in his own right and his record as a member of that memorable Leeds team of the sixties and early seventies stood as an example for everyone. A great player and intelligent manager, there was always a warm, caring tone in his voice and when he told me that all would be well, I felt relaxed and reassured and once again could look to the future.

One thing was clear, I had come back too soon and this time we took it easier. Again it meant more long afternoons of tiring muscle-building exercises, then to the next stage of running and feeling my way and as Christmas closed in, at last the chance to get back into the full swing of things.

When I was named in the first-team squad for the holiday games Christmas celebrations passed me by for about the first time I can ever remember. My chance came against Bristol City at the Hawthorns and I was there at left-back. I know a lot of players have trouble after a serious injury and although you try to sweep those worries away there's always a note of caution in the back of your mind. But any doubts I had soon disappeared because after a few games the old left leg was as good as ever, and I was determined to keep my place in the side.

That's it I thought, two broken legs is surely more than my fair share of injuries for a good few years and I could get on to build a future. Fortune could not have been kinder for me then, a hat-trick against title chasing Ipswich Town, a first appearance at Old Trafford and a call up to the England under-21 team which sadly I had to withdraw from because of Albion's league commitment.

But then my mind cleared and memories of those goals crashing in and of those newspaper headlines of that first hat-trick turned cold.

I was on the way to hospital again – Mam was trying to see if we were nearly there while Denise leaned forward. Still she was managing a smile and for a moment her words of encouragement warmed me.

The Robson family were a good sturdy lot after all and were never ones to turn away from a challenge. I had always been brought up to face problems head on and tackle them as best I could. Never feel sorry for yourself was advice I can still remember being drummed into us back at junior school in Chester-le-Street.

But threatening those thoughts now, were fears. What if a third broken leg is more than bad luck? Could there be a weakness somewhere which had gone undetected, and come to that how many players, good players, I mean, had come back from three broken legs in one season?

Dave Mackay, that old Spurs gladiator, was one who had suffered similar troubles – but not three breaks in one season. Was it all going to be too much?

My mind just kept spinning as we waited for the X-rays and then to have the plaster put on. Some thoughtful soul hardly raised the mood when she dashed in to say Albion had lost 2-0 to Manchester City. But then the doctor's initial examination wiped away some of my fears. It was a clean break, there was no apparent weakness. It was, he said, just bad luck.

Bad luck, I thought, how that can change your life. That night both John Giles and George Wright were round to see me. I was perched on the settee with my leg resting up and watching television or making a pretence by staring at the screen. My worries and fears were still bouncing around inside me and the chance to talk came as a welcome relief.

The manager was as calm and confident as ever and thoughtfully told me the best way to relax and plan for the future. The season was coming to an end anyway so there would be plenty of time ahead to get fit and ready. And George had already got my training schedule worked out.

For all their kind words I knew the next few months would not be all plain sailing. Everybody in and around the club would be watching me to see if I could overcome the physical and mental barriers. When I went out for a drink and a game of snooker with a few mates I recognized the look I got. All the people I met wanted to know how I was and when I would be back. At the club the local reporters would ask the same and yet all along I alone was asking the question that was on everybody's lips and yet no one would dare come out with. 'Is Bryan

Robson finished? There're better men than young Robson who've been beaten by such cruel fate.'

But as the stolen whispers and looks continued I knew that I could make it back. The medical advice was on my side, but what the hell . . . it was all down to me. It had taken a long haul to get to the first team of a first division club. My life had always been football and ever since I was twelve I had been working towards the chance to play on a great sporting stage. So many people had helped me and there was always Mam and Dad behind ready to come to the rescue. Twice that season I had come back from broken legs only to fall down again, but the third time would be the last.

Bryan Robson was not going to duck a challenge and anyway there were those medals and caps that tiny young lad from County Durham had promised his parents when they waved him off at the station all those years before.

# 2
## *Early Days*

First childhood memories are supposed to be important and significant in later life. And in my case that could not have been truer.

I was born and brought up in Witton Gilbert, a tidy little village just north of Durham. It was free from the sprawl of mines and yards that dominate Tyneside.

Our neat little semi in Front Street was a perfect home. My Dad, Brian, (I was named after him but had the 'y' instead of an 'i'), was a long distance lorry driver and would often be away for days at a time. That left my Mam, Maureen, to run the house and in the early days there was just me and my sister Sue, who was two years older. Younger brothers, Justin and Gary, arrived some years later.

Going back to those first memories, mine were, not surprisingly, of football. At weekends Dad would be home from his travels and my treat used to come on a Sunday. The only really clear picture I've still got of Witton Gilbert is of the hill that shadowed over the houses where on Sunday morning Dad would take Sue and me and Shane, our golden retriever, scrambling up for a game of football. Once at the top the ground flattened out and there was plenty of space to run.

Sue would always be the reluctant goalkeeper as Dad and I kicked around. He always encouraged me, and I'm told that he was a fair player himself in his day, although National Service put paid to any hopes he had of playing as a professional.

He would tease me by rolling the ball around with his

feet and to a five-year-old it was spellbinding. The ball moved faster than I could run and when finally Dad began to tire he would flick it to me and away I would go galloping across the grass.

Apart from the hill my other training ground was the sands at South Shields. In the summer we would pack up our lunch and Dad would drive us there for the day. The football was one way of keeping me quiet and out of mischief. On the windier days I must have covered every inch of that beach as the ball was whipped along the surface.

When I was six we moved from our council house in Witton Gilbert to a new house of our own in the South Pelaw district of Chester-le-Street. Dad had gone on to the longer and more lucrative continental trips and it was decided we could afford something better.

Chester-le-Street was only a few miles down the road from Witton Gilbert and although it meant a change of school there were no complaints from me. The move took us nearer Gran and the rest of the Robson family, and I'd also been promised there were more lads of my age to play with.

Mam was soon expecting Justin and because the mortgage was beginning to pinch, Dad decided to sell up and move to a council house on the nearby estate. It was a courageous decision to make because we could have afforded to stay on but Mam and Dad after plenty of heartsearching felt that too much money was going on the house and not enough was left to make life happy and easier for the family.

We moved just around the corner to Pelaw Road, South Pelaw, and that is still the Robson family home.

Dad was still working away a lot and Mam would be in charge. She was the one who kept us kids in line and would dish out the punishment where and when necessary.

It was my football that seemed to land me in trouble most. Like so many would-be footballers I would go out into the back garden and for hours on end kick and head the ball backwards and forwards against the wall.

Many great matches were played and many great goals scored as I hammered the ball around. The monotonous thud against the kitchen wall would drive Mam mad at times and more than once I'd be hauled in for an early tea or turned out to play on the green nearby.

The green was an important part of my football education, and come to that, my early days. Football matches on the green were full-blooded affairs. About twenty of us would gather after school and at weekends. There was a natural division between those of us who were Newcastle fans and those who carried the red and white of Sunderland. There was a local derby practically every day in South Pelaw on the green and we would have endless arguments and tussles.

With jumpers or coats for goal posts, the main problem was whether or not the ball had gone inside or outside the post, not to mention whether it was too high.

But for all the arguments we had some cracking games on that green and although it was all very basic kick and rush a few valuable lessons were learned.

In our matches I always played for Newcastle as the Robsons were United fans of many years standing. It was my Dad who had taken me to St James Park as a seven-year-old. The first match I can remember was against Northampton Town when both sides were in the second division. It stands out because it was just before Christmas, and both teams were in the running for promotion.

There were more people inside St James Park than I had ever seen in my life, and anyone who has been to Newcastle on such an occasion will know that enchanting atmosphere. The Liverpool and Manchester crowds take some beating but on Tyneside there is a different flavour. All the people seem to know their football inside out, and the knowledge and love of the game shines out.

There is so much tradition and football folklore in the North East that supporters like to think it is the true home of the sport. Tyneside has suffered so much over the years as one recession has bitten into another, and in those days most people looked to the football for not only enjoyment but also inspiration.

Another reason, and perhaps the main one, for remembering the Northampton game was that Newcastle hammered them 5-0. To be honest I haven't a clue who scored but my first impressions were of a chunky centre-forward called Ron McGarry whose strength and drive took my breath away. It was strange as well to see the name of Bryan Robson tucked away in the programme. Not me, of course, but Pop Robson who became one of the great Geordie footballing heroes.

When I was eight the following year and Newcastle were back in the first division we went to most of the home games. There would always be me and Dad, sometimes Sue came, and now and again Mam would join us, because she also liked her football. My proudest possessions were a black and white bobble hat and large wooden rattle which clanked into action. Sadly you don't see them at all these days but they were far more enjoyable, and come to that noisier, than the shouting of today.

We would try to get to the ground for around two o'clock and the rush would be on for a prized seat on the wall behind the advertising hoardings.

From that wall I saw all my early heroes, goalscorers mainly. The Manchester United trio of Law, Best and Charlton, then there were Greaves and Gilzean of Spurs and St John and Hunt of Liverpool. So many great players, but although I enjoyed them, my favourite was not surprisingly a Newcastle player – Wyn Davies.

To a small boy he was a giant of a man, Welshman Wyn. With a crew cut as short as a nail brush and the build of a weightlifter he was, in many ways, an effective leader of the United attack. What impressed me most was the way he would launch himself fearlessly forwards. I swear to this day that Wyn Davies could head a ball as hard as most could kick it. I can remember seeing him score with a header from the edge of the box. He was a yard above his centre half and that ball hit the back of the net with such venom . . . the goalkeeper hardly moved.

Newcastle has always loved its centre-forwards, the Milburns and Macdonalds, and to me then, the ultimate in life would have been to emerge in the black and white stripes from that tunnel at St James Park with the red number nine on my back.

Most Saturdays, I was playing football for the school in the morning, and off to St James Park in the afternoon, if United were playing at home.

Although my little world revolved around football, Mam always pushed Sue and me to do well at school. At Chester-le-Street junior school I was never top of the class but enjoyed the work. No matter how hard I tried though, the end of term report would usually go something like this:

'Bryan is a bright and active boy and if only he would direct the same amount of energy to his studies as he does to his football . . . then he would go far.'

As captain of the school football side, I was chosen for the Chester-le-Street junior schools team – my first representative game. But without doubt my finest hour came with the local cub pack. The cubs' football team was through to the semi-finals of the local knockout cup, and quite a few of my friends were in the side. They kept badgering me to join up, so that I could play with them and hopefully help the team on to the final.

With no ambitions at all to be one of Baden-Powell's happy wanderers I nevertheless volunteered to join the pack. The art of tying sheepshanks and running bowlines was way beyond me but I hadn't the heart to say that I was only really there to play in the football team.

We won the semi-final and in the final hammered the opposition 11-0 and the Cup was ours. Bob Heslby, a famous amateur player in those parts, presented us with our medals.

That was just about the sum total of my scouting career, although I can remember going on a summer camp in Kent before quietly hanging up my cap and woggle.

Having failed the eleven plus, I started a new school, the Birtley South First Senior School, but that soon changed as the area went comprehensive and I began to settle down at the Lord Lawson School. It was here my football really began to flourish.

The PE teacher was Bill Chapman and to him I owe an awful lot. He was a stocky, well built man who loved his sport, and took great delight in his football teams doing well. As captain of the junior team and a regular member of the under-14 side I was coming along well and enjoying it all immensely.

At that age came my first thoughts of being a footballer and my ambitions were fuelled by a knock at the front door one night.

It was one of those moments that will be preserved for ever in my mind. We had just finished tea, Sue and I were helping Mam clear the table, Dad was flicking through the paper whilst younger brothers Justin and Gary played on the floor. The door bell went and Mam bustled off to see who it was.

'There's a man to see us about Bryan,' she announced, and a thickset chap in an old mackintosh was ushered into the room. For a moment my heart raced as I tried to think what I'd done wrong.

Birdnesting was one of our more adventurous pastimes and perhaps he had seen us clambering over somebody's garden wall or fence. For the life of me I could not think what he wanted.

Then he looked towards me and gave a broad, encouraging sort of smile which settled me down again. He sat on the settee and started to explain.

'It's the young lad. I've been watching him play football for the school team and you know there's an awful lot of potential there.'

The stranger glanced towards my parents to see them still mystified as to what he actually wanted.

'Well,' he went on, 'I do some scouting for Burnley and your Bryan is just the sort of lad they're interested in. I know it's still early days but they'd like to have a closer look at him. I don't want to raise your hopes too high,' he said, as he flicked his attention towards me. 'But I reckon he might just have the makings and it's worth encouraging.'

I didn't dare say anything and looked towards Mam and Dad who were looking at each other for an answer.

It was Dad who did the talking from then on and he promised the scout we would give his offer some careful thought. Dad explained I was only twelve, so it was some time yet before any major decision on my future had to be made. But Dad explained that if Burnley wanted to offer me some sort of trial then it would be all right.

Well that night I was buzzing. I just couldn't concentrate on anything and my mind was awash with dreams of football. It must be one of the most exciting things that has ever happened to me and it was a difficult job getting to sleep.

I lay in bed staring at the walls which were plastered with mementoes – Newcastle team groups, my heroes like George Best and the colourful pennants that Dad always brought back from his foreign travels, names like Juventus and Real Madrid lined the bedroom walls and that night I played in the Cup Final, the European Cup Final and the World Cup Final all before I finally dozed off.

I woke early, got dressed and bounced down the stairs, only to be lectured over breakfast by Mam.

'Now I don't want you bragging about that Burnley chap at school today, young man,' she warned.

'No, Mam, I won't, honest' . . . What a lie!

I couldn't get to school fast enough that day and once in the playground it was impossible not to broadcast about my new found fame. Most of my mates were chuffed, although naturally one or two were a little envious.

After Burnley several other local scouts called at the house and soon there was quite a list. Newcastle, West Bromwich Albion, Leeds, Coventry, Middlesbrough, Sunderland and Arsenal all wanted me to go for trials, but there was still a long way to go.

Two other major landmarks stand out whilst I was at school. My first major cup win and my first sending off, which cost me a caning.

The sending off came in a school practice match one afternoon. Although billed as a friendly the going was getting pretty fierce and the games master blew for a foul against me. For no real reason other than sheer frustration I hoofed the ball away in temper. The whistle went again, he strode across and showing all the action you would expect from a first division referee, pointed towards the changing rooms.

'Right, Robson, you're off. But you're going to pay for it and you can run round the pitch until you've got rid of that temper of yours,' he barked at me.

So off I went jogging around the touchline. A good twenty minutes went by and there I was still pounding around the pitch. The game was still going on and the master showed no interest in me. Well, to be honest, I was tired and fed up and thought, wrongly, as it turned out, that they had forgotten about me. So when I was at one end and play was at the other I started to walk and straightaway the shrill of the whistle made me look up.

And there was the master running towards me, his finger waving. I was told to report to the headmaster and my first football fine amounted to two very painful whacks across the bottom with the cane. It makes me wonder today when they have so much trouble in schools and at football matches – perhaps we are too soft these days. That punishment taught me a lesson and I've never been sent off since.

If that was an unhappy memory, a golden one came at the end of the season. I was captain of the Washington and District team and we had fought our way through to the final of the local Hartlepool Hospital Cup Competition. Our opponents in the final were Darlington.

The final was played at Sacriston, on the local miners' welfare ground and to us this was a real challenge. The pitch was rolled flat, the white lines had been specially done and with goalnets and corner flags it was going to be our Wembley. To add to the occasion a crowd of around two hundred lined the pitch to watch. All the family were there to cheer me on and the locals did us proud by turning out in force as well.

I must admit leading the team out in front of a crowd for the first time was a nerve-racking experience, and it took both sides time to settle down. We played well that day and in the end were worthy winners at 2-0. The cup was ours and just as I was about to go up and receive the trophy one of the teachers came across and told me to say a few words of thanks and also commiserate with the losers.

At first I froze as the crowd huddled round. Waiting with the cup was one of the officials from the local FA. I shuffled forward, took the cup and then turned to see all those expectant faces staring at me. A jumble of words came spurting out as I thanked the official for the cup and called for three cheers for the losers. My ordeal was over and we could enjoy our cup win.

All this time scouts from different clubs kept calling at the house or writing, and when I was thirteen the next step forward came, a week on trial during the holidays with West Bromwich Albion. Although I was looking forward to it I was also frightened at the thought of being on my own away from home. There was no need to worry because Mam and Dad took me to the station and there we met up with one of the Albion scouts, Norman Humphreys, whose job it was to look us over. Norman was an easy-going, jovial sort of chap and I soon felt at ease with him. There was a group of six from the area going down and with me was one of my pals, John Waugh, another veteran of those matches on the local green.

What a week it turned out to be. Arriving in Birmingham we were taken to the Cobden Hotel on the Hagley Road. It was the first hotel I had ever stopped in on my own and we had a room between two of us.

John and I shared, and imagine the thoughts of two young lads down from the north east in a large luxury hotel. We were looked after like royalty and from that first week as a thirteen-year-old on trial I was impressed with the Albion.

They were not the grandest or most successful of clubs, but they were friendly and extremely kind and that's something I will never forget. We trained every morning and most afternoons as well. In the evening we either went to watch a local match or were taken to the pictures. We went to see the musical 'Hair', which in those days was a little bit naughty. This was one visit I wouldn't be telling Mam about, I can remember thinking to myself.

That week of coaching and training left us all exhausted. It was six weary lads who made the journey back north. But a week of taking in the thrilling atmosphere of a football club had affected all of us. I had gone to Birmingham to see what I thought of the club and I was going back convinced more than ever that I wanted to be a footballer.

On the advice of my Dad and good old Bill Chapman at school, I had similar weeks with Coventry and Burnley. Neither lived up to Albion though. At Burnley we were left to fend for ourselves too much, while at Coventry there was just something about the club that did not suit. I also went to Newcastle for a trial and it's funny really, although I loved the club so much, there was something at the back of me that kept pushing towards West Bromwich Albion.

It must have been mutual because one day soon afterwards, Alan Ashman, who was manager of Albion then, and chief scout Paddy Ryan 'phoned to see if they could call and discuss my future.

When they called, Mam and Dad and myself sat and listened to what they had to say. At the age of thirteen they wanted me to sign schoolboy forms with them which would mean that for the next two years at least, I would be tied to the Hawthorns. The decision was mine, both Mam and Dad were happy to go along with what I wanted, and they were satisfied that Albion would treat me as fairly as any other club would. So Albion it was.

The next two years saw my football develop and during the holidays there were regular trips to the Midlands to train with Albion. My pal, John Waugh, had not made the grade so I was on my own, but I teamed up with another Chester-le-Street lad, David Holden, who was older than me. He was my guardian angel if you like, and we shared digs together during the holidays. I was given the grand sum of £5 a week expenses. At first I thought I had struck it rich but by the time I'd paid for lunches and 'bus fares to and from the ground there was not much left. What was left paid for the occasional trip to the pictures or the local pitch and putt course on the park.

During term time it was Bill Chapman who kept me going. He volunteered to help, and how valuable he was. Twice a week he would give up his time after school, and the two of us would get together in the gym. Bill devised special training and weight circuits for me, and it was just the sort of boost I needed. To have a teacher like Bill Chapman, was perhaps one of the luckiest breaks I ever had. He always took an interest, and was proud to see one of his lads forging a career in football. I like to think that my progress and success in the game reflects back on Bill Chapman. We still keep in touch today, and I know that I will never be able to thank him enough for all he did.

As so often happens in football, while I had been gradually plodding on in Chester-le-Street, there had been changes at the Albion. Alan Ashman, the manager who had signed me on schoolboy forms was gone, and his place taken by Don Howe, one of the architects behind the fabulous Arsenal side that did the double.

Happily, the change at the top did not affect my future and after two years on schoolboy forms the time had come for Albion to make up their minds about me. It was in the summer of 1972 and I was fifteen. I'd spent the holidays training with the club's youth team and it was after one session that the call to the manager's office came. To youngsters like myself, the manager's office was akin to the headmaster's study.

At Albion, Don Howe had a tiny little place buried under the main stand. There were no windows and daylight could only seep in through the glass panels in the partition wall.

There was just enough room for the desk, a filing cabinet and three chairs. When I was called in, Don Howe was sitting at the desk and also there was chief scout Paddy Ryan, who two years previously had signed me on schoolboy forms.

The meeting was brief. I was offered the chance to join Albion as an apprentice professional. The pay was £8 a week, but that was neither here nor there. What did matter was that I had taken the next step.

I didn't float out of the office on cloud nine, because with the signing, came a word of caution from Don Howe. He stressed that for the next two years I would be on trial. It was still up to me to show the club I had a future.

'Remember only a few of the lads we sign here actually make it all the way to the first team. We'll give you everything we've got, but you've got to do the same,' warned Howe.

So I was all set for a move to the Midlands. Those training weeks in the summer had given me more confidence and I was less dependent on home. But when the time came to leave Mam and Dad and set off for good, I was a little apprehensive at what lay ahead.

# 3
## *The Apprenticeship*

It was a burning hot July day when we drove down from Chester-le-Street to Birmingham. All six of us were packed in the car, and it was a real family day out. Mam and Dad insisted on driving me down. I think they wanted to put their minds at rest by seeing where I'd be living. My home for the next eighteen months was to be in digs, with a lady called Mrs Curtis. She lived on her own in a spotless little semi, in an area called Hampstead, which was about a ten minute bus ride from the Hawthorns ground.

I was given a double bedroom upstairs. Nothing elaborate. It had a double bed, an old chair, a chest of drawers, and a wardrobe which easily took all my belongings. There was a television in the lounge downstairs and Mrs Curtis gave me a free run of her home. She was in her sixties, a slight woman, who was always very kind and pleasant and tremendously house-proud. Everything had its place, and if it was not in it, then there would be trouble. It was more than my life's worth to leave papers or shoes lying around, and I made sure I always obeyed the one golden house rule of keeping everything immaculate.

In the mornings I would make the bed, leave the curtains straight and tidy everything away. It was hard at first, but looking back it was all good discipline and thanks to dear old Mrs Curtis my life has been a tidy one ever since. I owe her a lot because, unbeknown to me, when I first arrived, she was to play the most important role of all in my early football career. I'd imagined that I would be set to work by Albion, training hard and fighting for a place in the junior teams. But when the day came to report officially for pre-season training, there was quite a shock in store for me.

I lined up with the small group of newly-signed apprentices in the dressing room. We all looked more like young soldiers waiting for their first inspection, than a group of budding footballers. With our chests stuck out and hands by our sides we were welcomed by Don Howe, the manager, and Albert McPherson, who was then the youth team trainer. Albert was to be our real boss, and both he and the manager gave us a rundown of what they expected from us. The club rules were read out and none of us was left under any illusions. Although we were there to play football and enjoy ourselves, we were also expected to behave and respect the good name of the club.

The next task was the measuring ceremony and this had been worrying me. Most of the other lads were a lot bigger and broader, and for some reason I'd stopped growing. I was only 4 feet 11 inches tall and weighed 6 stones, which for a fifteen-year-old footballer was not much good. When I got to the scales that morning, Albert McPherson studied the weight closely and then looked me up and down. He was clearly a little worried, and after a few moments, outlined his thoughts.

'Well Bryan lad, we're going to have to build you up if we're going to make anything of you. A few more inches and a couple of stones will be more good for you than any practice matches, if you want to make it.'

So, from that morning I was set aside from the rest of the newcomers. The club gave me a mountain of paper about what to eat and drink, and what exercises to do at home. The club trainers made it clear that before I could concentrate on polishing up and learning more football skills I had to get myself in shape. And this is where Mrs Curtis came to the rescue. She was an extremely good cook, and, having had lodgers from the Albion before, knew what was needed.

Next morning the bodybuilding commenced. First came a concoction which contained a raw egg, beaten in with some milk, sugar and a tot of sherry. The first day it was hard to swallow, especially when she told me what it was. It took me back to when I was small and faced with a dose of cough mixture or ghastly medicine. Mam always made me gulp it down. 'The quicker it goes down, the quicker the taste has gone,' she would say. So down the hatch went the glass of yellowish slimy mixture. Next there was the cereal which was usually followed by a cooked breakfast washed down with tea. 'An army marches on its stomach,' were Mrs Curtis' parting words of a morning. At first it felt as though I'd eaten the entire army's rations for a whole week, and early morning training was a difficult chore at first with so much extra food inside me.

There was a lunchtime snack of a sandwich or some chips from the supporters' club next to the ground, and then came the evening meal. A large round plate piled high with food would be brought to the dining room by Mrs Curtis, who must have had about a tenth of what I did.

There was always plenty of vegetables and the thickest steaks or largest meat pies you could ever wish to see. I ploughed through the dinner hoping it would have the same effect on me as a tin of spinach had on Popeye. Quite often I would weigh myself on the bathroom scales, or measure myself against the door frame to see if Mrs Curtis' dinners were building me up. Slowly but surely it was working. The food I enjoyed, but the thing I really hated was the drink.

It's not often that a football club recommends its players to drink, but on the Albion diet sheet there were strict instructions. I was to have a glass of stout every night with my dinner. Well, now and again I enjoyed a glass of shandy or half a lager, but stout was definitely not my drink. Mrs Curtis would carefully pour the bottle into a glass, making sure there was a rich creamy head on the jet black beer. It's a good thing the dinners were tasty because I would close my eyes, take a breath, gulp down a few mouthfuls of stout and then cram some food in quickly before the taste of the beer hit me. I would think of that old television advert with a chap supping his stout and saying 'It looks good, tastes good and by golly it does you good.' Rather him than me. A glass of stout was an ordeal and I hated it. More than once in the early days I felt like tipping it into one of Mrs Curtis' flower vases and letting the daffodils feel the benefit instead. The glass sitting in front of me every night did not look very appetizing, the taste was questionable, but the goodness must have worked.

After four or five months of Mrs Curtis' steaks and meat pies and a few crates of stout Bryan Robson was on the way up and spreading out. I had grown around three or four inches and put on nearly two stones. When I first arrived that summer Albion had been seriously worried about my weight, and one of the trainers had even suggested I was too small for a professional footballer. But now I had made up the ground, and what a relief it was the morning I was weighed, measured and given the thumbs up by the trainers.

The life of a young footballer is not as easy or as golden as most think. In the mornings you have to be at the ground for 9.30 at the latest, and after getting changed there are usually a few odd jobs to do. Sometimes I helped in the first-team dressing room by getting the kit ready or making a huge pot of tea for them. There were balls to blow up and errands to run before the juniors would climb into the mini-bus and make for the training ground about a mile away. We trained together most of the time, although every now and then there was a chance to play with the reserves, or if you were really lucky, with the first team.

England centre-forward Jeff Astle, his goalscoring partner Tony Brown, and the Scottish international midfield player Asa Hartford were the big names at the time. Bobby Gould, that bustling and bubbly little man, was there for a spell before moving on to Bristol City, and, just before Christmas, a buzz went round the club. The first team had been struggling, and were near the bottom of the first division. One morning I picked up the paper to read that they had paid out a club record fee of £135,000 to Glasgow Rangers for winger Willie Johnston – it was a record for a Scottish league player – and little did I think then that this international star would help create one of my most treasured soccer memories – my first goal in league football. That was still in the future, the first-teamers were names to look up to, and also, clean up after. After training every day, the apprentices would have to collect all the kit, take it to be washed, and brush down the dressing rooms. Boots would have to be cleaned and polished, left hanging by their heels on the giant board ready for another day, and it was often a welcome relief when everywhere was spick and span.

Most nights I stayed in and either read upstairs in my bedroom or watched the television downstairs with Mrs Curtis. Now and again a group of us would go for a game of snooker or to the pictures, but I was happy staying in most of the time. I don't think Mrs Curtis was, because she would often ask me why I did not go out more, in a tone which implied she was a bit fed up of me hanging around. All in all those were happy days with Mrs Curtis, but life there came to a strange end. Although she pushed me to go out more, she was most insistent that if I did go out, I was back before midnight, so the house could be locked up. Well, one Saturday night after a youth team game, a gang of us went down to a disco in West Bromwich. A good time was being had by all and the time simply escaped me. We stayed until the music died and the lights dimmed and by the time I made it home it was half past two. Walking up the road I could see the house was in total darkness, not even the hall light was on. Carefully opening and closing the gate I slid the key out of my pocket and slipped it into the lock. But as I turned and pushed to get in, I bumped against the door as nothing happened. The door was obviously locked from the inside. With just a glimmer of hope that Mrs Curtis might have left the back door open or on the latch, I crept around to find out. No luck, everywhere was locked and the windows all shut tight. My window was open slightly but after a few drinks there was no way I was going shinning up drain pipes. I wandered back around the front and began to panic. I daren't ring the bell because Mrs Curtis would blow her top, and all my friends lived a good distance away. Happily not everybody in Woodford Road was in bed. From across the road came a chap in shirt sleeves and carpet slippers. I'd often passed the time of day with him because he was an Albion fan and would often ask me about the team and the goings on at the club.

'What's up lad? Has she locked you out?' he said, half whispering and half shouting.

'I'm afraid so, yes. Everywhere's locked and there are no windows open,' was my rather forlorn reply.

'Well, come over to us if you've got nowhere to go and kip on our sofa,' was the heartwarming response.

So that night, I slept in the house opposite. The next morning when I tried, nonchalantly, to wander into Mrs Curtis' as though nothing had happened, she was there waiting for me. There was no scene or violent telling off, because she knew, that I knew, I had broken the rules. I was not given my marching orders, but both of us realized that perhaps a parting of the ways would be for the better. My aunt and uncle lived in Birmingham, and I considered asking them if I could stay with them. But they lived too far from the ground and I also wanted to stand up for myself, away from the family. They had some friends though, who were nearer the ground and were keen to take in a lodger. Ron and Irene Hinton and their son Peter, who was four years younger than me, lived over at Great Barr, which was handy for the ground and they very kindly offered me a room.

Although Mrs Curtis had looked after me in grand style, I enjoyed the move, because going to Ron and Irene's was like returning home to Chester-le-Street. They treated me as one of their own, and Ron became a good friend. Despite my lockout escapade, I was not a great one for going out, because my football came first. But Ron brought me out of my shell more, and once a week we would go down to his local for a drink and a game of darts or dominoes. I enjoyed a break from the football club every now and again, although there was no real escape of course. Most of Ron's neighbours and friends were Albion supporters and they always wanted to talk about the way the team was playing.

That first season at the Hawthorns there was little joy for the supporters, as the side struggled near the bottom of the division. In the end they finished up twenty-second and that meant relegation and second division football. Towards the end of my first season, however, things were looking brighter for me. I was in the junior team that played in the Midland Youth League. The bodybuilding course had worked well, and I was holding my own, switching between defence and midfield, the role I enjoyed best.

Although relegation did not directly affect the juniors and apprentices, you could feel a cloud of despair fall over the club. There were a few long faces in the first-team dressing room, and to be honest, there were moments when I wondered if I had joined the right club. But a pep talk from Don Howe, who managed to hide his intense disappointment, lifted me. He told everyone at the club that as far as he was concerned Albion would still be considered as a first division side, and the drop down to the second was just a temporary lapse.

'There'll be no cutbacks or drastic changes. We will come back stronger than ever,' were Don Howe's last words to the players before they all disappeared for the summer break.

It was good that summer to spend a few weeks back home and I did not realize how much I had missed it until I arrived back there. The games were still going strong on the green although the players looked younger and smaller, but nothing had really changed. It was still Newcastle against Sunderland and the black and whites were on top. I went back to school to see Bill Chapman, who was eagerly awaiting my end of season report. As always, he listened intently and then chipped in with his useful bits of advice. Back home, Dad was still working as hard as ever and Justin, who was now nine, and seven-year-old Gary were bursting with life. They were both football mad and most of my time was taken up with endless games of soccer and cricket. Another major step forward came with a summer tour to Germany with the Albion youth team. We played in an annual festival in Augsburg against a host of other youth teams from all over Europe.

One vital factor missing from my game before then was confidence. At school and in junior matches nothing had ever worried me, but in that first season at Albion, it had not been easy. I got off to a late start because of my size, and had spent more time working on fitness programmes than football skills. Quite often in the afternoon I would go in for extra training, sometimes on my own, just to practise simple things like shooting, passing and ball control. In Germany the extra training paid off. The team played well and for the first time at Albion, my confidence was there. I was looking for the ball and battling for it, rather than standing off and letting someone else get in front.

Albert McPherson, the youth team coach, took me aside after the tournament to encourage me even more. Any doubts I had about making the grade, were washed completely out of my mind in Germany, and when the time came for pre-season training again, I strode into the Hawthorns feeling ten feet tall. I was determined to show the coaches what I was capable of, and I had to, because that season they would have to decide whether to sign me on as a full-time professional.

During that second season I established myself as a regular in the youth team, and we had a good year. John Osborne, one of the bravest and most underrated goalkeepers there has ever been, was on a part-time basis with the club and he often played with us in the Midland Youth League. 'Ossy' was a marvellous man to have in the team. We used to pull his leg about being the oldest man in the side, but his experience was just what we wanted. We won the league and the Midland cup that year and another great player to grace the side was Jeff Astle. He was on his way back from injury and to be honest, was not the player he had been. Despite that, the thrill of playing with Jeff was quite something. He was one of the favourites with the fans, who still cherished his winning goal in the 1968 Cup Final against Everton. If Jeff was in our youth team a few more people would come along and watch. Although he was a yard slower than the thrusting youngsters around him, Jeff could play some delightful football. He would let the ball do the work and we all admired his timing and finishing. Playing with men such as Ossy and Jeff made me realize how much more there was to learn about the game before I could rightfully challenge for a place in the first team.

My first real chance at Albion came in the reserve team towards the end of the season. I was named to play left back against Everton reserves at Goodison Park in the Central league. On the way up we stopped for a pre-match meal and Bill Asprey, who was then coach, gave the team talk. My instructions were to take it easy, not to commit myself too much and to keep as close to my man as possible. I'd enjoyed the journey up and the stop for a meal, but when the team bus pulled up in front of Goodison Park a queasy feeling started in my stomach. Nerves were not something that usually bothered me, but it was that first day at school feeling. Everybody else looked so assured and at ease and I tried to give the impression that I was too. The hour before a game is always the worst. It's the only time when nerves can get the better of you and sitting in that Goodison Park dressing room that day, that hour stretched for ever. I tied and untied my boot laces about half a dozen times, adjusted my shin pads and kicked the ball against the wall. Looking round, the rest of the lads were full of confidence, Joe Mayo, John Trewick and Barry Donaghy and Bill Bulloch, (two lads who floated out of soccer a little later), were laughing and joking.

The bell for the teams finally went and we were off. If anything, emerging from the Goodison tunnel was an anti-climax, the loudspeaker was making more noise than the crowd, who were few and far between. Once the whistle went, I settled down and the nerves disappeared. I didn't have a great deal to do, but even so noticed that everything and everybody was moving a pace faster than I was used to. The few things I had to do, I managed. It was in the second half that my memorable moment came. Everton pumped a long ball from defence and I chased after it. There was not another player in sight at the time and I decided to let the ball run out for a throw. A shout from the side warned me there was a man closing in. That someone was big Joe Royle. He was only in the reserves making a comeback after injury, and when I flicked my head round there he was bearing down fast. I tried to shield the ball and let it run out, but Joe had different ideas. He sent me flying as he barged into me. I went slithering and sliding onto the cinder track that surrounds the pitch and my arms and legs were a mass of cuts and grazes. Bill Asprey came running up and the cold water sponge stung as he washed away the dirt. Digging into his bag, Bill brought out three or four rolls of bandage and proceeded to wrap these round my wounds. By the time he finished I looked like the invisible man with bandages all over. We won the game 2-1 but back in the dressing room Bill was waiting for me with a complaint.

'Look here young Bryan, if you're going to get cut up like this every match, you'll cost us a fortune. We'll have to get a new medical kit every week.'

All the lads laughed, and that night, my reserve team debut was celebrated back in West Bromwich with a few pints in the town pubs. Come next morning, I can remember thinking that I would not be able to take many more debuts like that.

In August 1974 the call to the manager's office came. Don Howe was still in charge, and when I walked into his office a contract was sitting on his desk; my contract as a professional footballer. The pay was £28 a week, and I could not sign it quick enough. It was five years since that scout had come knocking at the door, and now I was there. With the contract came a signing-on fee of £250. I must have read the figures on that cheque a hundred times. I'd never seen so much money in my life, and after training that morning, I made for the nearest telephone box. I couldn't wait to tell Mam the news, and shouting down the phone I told her of the contract and the bumper signing-on fee. Although tempted to go out and have a spend, caution got the better of me, and I trooped down to the local building society to open an account. On the way, I kept putting my hand into my pocket to make sure the cheque was still there, and it was a proud moment when I handed it over the counter.

The following season I was a regular in the reserve team and on Fridays I would glance at the noticeboard in the dressing room, half hoping that my name might just be on the first-team sheet instead.

A run of disappointing results through March had cost Albion a promotion place and one Monday morning the club was busier than usual. Reporters were hanging around the office and there was talk in the dressing room of a special board meeting to discuss the future. Speculation was rife that Don Howe's job was in jeopardy and in the afternoon it was confirmed in a radio sports bulletin. The directors had decided not to renew the manager's contract when it expired at the end of the season, and Don Howe had decided to quit there and then. I was sorry because he'd always been fair with me and would never miss the chance to offer words of encouragement. Perhaps he was a better coach than manager. He wished all the players well before leaving and there was a feeling in me that our paths would cross again sometime in the future. If only we'd known then that that sometime would be with the England team then our smiles could have been broader and our handshakes firmer.

# 4
# *The Baptism*

'As one door shuts another opens,' is a phrase I've heard used so many times around football clubs. Different managers bring fresh ideas and changes to a team. After all, they are the ones who are either canonized or slain by the game. The sudden departure of Don Howe from West Bromwich opened the way for reserve team trainer Brian Whitehouse to take over in a caretaker role. Brian was one of those chaps who easily melted into the background. He was, and still is, of course, a first-class coach who knows what he wants and usually gets it. I suppose you could say he's a players' man. A person who knows the game from top to bottom and goes about his job quietly and efficiently. It must have been a challenge for him to be pitched in at the helm. The press boys, and come to that some of the supporters, were asking 'Brian who?' But the directors made it pretty clear that his stay at the top would be only temporary until a bigger name could be found. The caretaker manager's job has got to be one of the most thankless tasks there is. You are expected to throw everything into it, and then gracefully step down when a new man arrives. In every caretaker there must be the hope that, if things were to go well, you could be rewarded with the job permanently.

Whatever thoughts Brian Whitehouse had, he went about his business in a determined fashion. His reign as chief was possibly going to be a short one, with only three matches left to the end of the season, but he was going to make his mark. Brian was a local man and over the months in the reserves I had come to respect his judgement and advice. That first week Brian immersed himself with the senior team and the reserves were left to train with the younger players. With the close of the season so near and promotion out of the question an end of term feeling was descending on the Hawthorns. On Friday morning though, Brian Whitehouse shook things up. There had been hints all week of changes in the first team and after training the side to play York City at Bootham Crescent was pinned on the dressing room noticeboard. There at number 10, was the name of Bryan Robson . . . my first team chance had come.

Brian did not say a lot to me that Friday, other than he thought I deserved my opportunity, and he wanted to freshen up the first team with new faces. My main concern was making sure my boots were packed in with all the other kit, and then running down to the phone box on the corner to spread the news to the family back home.

Saturday April 12 1975 is a date that will always be fixed in my mind. I did not sleep much the night before, and welcomed the early morning call from landlady Irene. She and Ron saw me off and I was first to arrive at the ground to catch the team bus north. Mam and Dad were driving down from home to see the game. On the way there I tried to read the papers and concentrate on a round of cards but it was mighty difficult. I could not get the game out of my mind, and some of the older players went out of their way to make me feel more at ease, by cracking jokes and talking non-stop, but I think they realized my mind was elsewhere. Bootham Crescent ground in York is best described as one of soccer's outposts. More people were visiting the Minster that day than making their way through the cramped streets to watch their local football team. Albion supporters were thin on the ground as well, because only the die-hards had bothered to travel north. It was so quiet when we pulled into the car park, that for one moment I thought the match had been called off.

In the dressing room the shirts were laid out at the pegs, and before getting changed there was a chance to snatch a quick word with my parents outside. Both were full of encouragement and Dad kidded me that York were no match for a Robson, especially on his first-team debut.

I played in midfield and it was hard at first to adjust to the pace. A question always asked is 'What difference is there between reserve and first-team football?' Well, I found out that day, and spent most of the game running and chasing hard. It helped with the team playing well, and my Dad was right as usual – York were no match for us. We won 3-1 and although I'd enjoyed my first game I was relieved to hear the whistle. All I could think of was resting my weary legs. I'd run myself practically into the ground, but everyone seemed satisfied with me back in the dressing room. I had not really had an awful lot to do, but most of the passes had been on target and the tackles had been won.

I was pleased for Brian too. It was the side's first away win since Christmas and his team changes had worked. The next morning I was down earlier than usual to read the verdicts of the Sunday papers. I got a mention in one, which spoke of my promising debut, and out came the kitchen scissors to snip the report out. Ron started pulling my leg, saying he didn't want his paper cut into ribbons every day, but the report was duly despatched to Mam who had ordered me to send her any mentions for inclusion in the family scrapbook which she kept.

The following Sunday there were even more cuttings, after my home debut against Cardiff City. This time I wore the number four shirt and just ten minutes had gone when Willie Johnston worked the ball down the wing. It floated across, the Cardiff defence dithered, and I kept running towards the ball. The full-back failed to clear, the goalkeeper was jumping up and down shouting furiously at his defence as it came to me. I was only six yards out and a firm boot would do it. Feeling the thunder of the Welsh defenders coming from the side, I swung, lashed at the ball and thankfully it went crashing into the net. The sense of achievement was quite something. Never before had I been so thrilled and overtaken by emotions. Running towards the Albion supporters I jumped and punched the air with jubilation. They were jumping up and down in celebration, and for the first time the name of Bryan Robson began to ring round the Hawthorns. It took me a good few minutes to collect myself but a thumping challenge from one of the Cardiff midfield men, which sent me tumbling over, finally did the trick.

The goal gave me confidence and for the second week running we won with the score 2-0. Afterwards a new hurdle awaited. Reporters wanted to ask me about the game and the goal. Who was I? Where had I come from? I mumbled out a few answers when they trapped me outside the dressing room and was surprised to see them in print the next day. Poor old Ron's papers took a battering that day as I combed the columns. One had even made me man of the match, which in only my second game was very flattering. It was disappointing the next week when the final game of the season came along. I was so enjoying my new role, that another few months would have suited me fine. Luckily, there was something else to look forward to. I had been chosen for the England Youth Squad to travel to Switzerland to play in the so called Mini World Cup.

Before that, however, the last game of the season at Nottingham Forest brought a mixture of elation and disappointment. I scored again but Albion lost 2-1; an eventful season had finished on a high note for me. Three games and two goals was not a bad record to go out on, and I hoped it would prove to be the foundation for the next season. The summer games with the England Youth Squad were immense fun and marvellous experience. Although it was only a youth team, there was still a tingle of excitement going through me as I pulled on an England shirt for the first time. We won the cup beating Finland in the final 1-0. Alongside me in the youth team were Glen Hoddle, Ray Wilkins and Peter Barnes. These three players were big names and rightly, our victories were greeted warmly back home as showing hope for the future.

While I was away that summer I kept hearing rumours, or reading reports in the papers, about who Albion were going to get as their new manager. One or two names were mentioned but the favourite was Johnny Giles of Leeds United. I was back home when the news came that Giles had got the job as player-manager. His record with Leeds was an impressive one, and the club was getting a highly skilled player as well as a manager. It did occur to me, of course, that the competition for midfield places would hot up but the pre-season training was only a few weeks away so I decided to make the most of my holidays.

Thanks to Ron I was now able to get about under my own steam. He had taught me to drive and some of the signing-on fee of £250 went on my first car, an old Chrysler. It was a real banger and at Albion they reckoned they could hear me coming ten minutes before I actually got there. The Chrysler did not last long, and was soon replaced by my parents' treasured black Austin Westminster, which I bought off them when they decided to get something newer. That car had the presence of a Rolls-Royce; the engine was so quiet that often when I was waiting at traffic lights or a junction, I would think the car had stalled. Sometimes I clanked the starter again, or put my foot on the accelerator to test the car and would roar forward. Inside, the seats were like armchairs, it was as comfy as our front room. The car had served my parents well. In seven years nothing had gone wrong, they had not even had a puncture. That's what made me buy it in the first place. A good old reliable car . . . a family friend. Whether it was the change of scenery or driver, I don't know, but that car never took to me! The very first week I had a puncture, and then three weeks later a group of us went into Birmingham for a night out. I parked it carefully in the street and locked up. But when I came to go home, it was nowhere to be seen – the old Robson Westminster had been pinched. It was a hard job telling Mam and Dad about the car, but they took it well, and even joked that the motor had probably got fed up with me and the Midlands, and driven itself back home to them. But the next day the old car turned up. Some joyriders had taken it and dumped it, but the radio and even the battery had been stolen.

In the summer apart from my flirtation with cars I also moved from Ron and Irene's, to a flat of my own nearby. It was a modest little place but I felt I was just about ready to look after myself. Help was not far away, because I was going out with a local girl called Denise. She lived a few roads away and we first met in the local pub. I was there having a quiet drink with two mates and Denise was with a group of friends celebrating a twenty-first birthday. We just got chatting over a drink. Denise was no football fan, and it made a pleasant change to talk about something other than Albion. I enjoyed her company so much the first night, that I plucked up courage to ask her out. When I moved to the flat, she volunteered to come in and clean once a week, and her mum, Doreen, did my washing. One of the first ordeals for any young man is to be taken to meet his girlfriend's parents, but what a greeting I got.

Denise's mum, knowing that I was with the Albion, turned to her husband George and said 'Never mind dear – he might get a decent job in the future!' To that, there was no answer! But they turned out to be a great couple and have always made me most welcome. As our friendship grew it was another car, of all things, that nearly came between us in those early days. Mine was in for repair and I'd borrowed Denise's mini to go to the ground. Taking extra care with it, I parked the car outside the ground and checked twice to make sure everything was locked. I was only there for about ten or fifteen minutes and was on the way out when one of the ground staff told me I was wanted in reception. Waiting for me there was a lorry driver, he was pacing up and down wringing his hands.

'It's your mini outside isn't it?' he said. I was just about to explain when he stumbled on. 'Well I'm sorry I didn't think I was that close to it. There's not that much damage and if I give you my name and insurance, we can sort it out from there. I'm very sorry, it was just one of those things,' he confessed. 'One of those things,' I thought to myself, he has gone and smashed the car. I ran out to inspect the damage and my heart sank, as I saw the crumpled wing and flaking paint on the driver's side. After exchanging names and numbers with the lorry driver I realized I was late to pick up Denise, who'd been horse riding. Driving along I started to wonder how to break the news. I must have rehearsed about ten different ways but before I'd had time to settle on the right one, there was Denise standing on the pavement waving me down. The funny thing was that from her side she couldn't see the damage and the first thing I got was a telling off for being ten minutes late. We drove off and I started to tell her about the lorry and the accident. Instead of anger there was disbelief. Because she could not see the damage from the passenger seat, she thought I was joking. It wasn't until we arrived home that the damaging truth hit her. I must admit she took it well, although, from then on, Denise was a bit wary whenever I asked to borrow the car. I made it up to her finally though, with one of the best days out we had in those early days. It was Grand National week and I had two tickets for Aintree on the Thursday.

A few days before the trip, I happened to be chatting to a pal, Charlie Chaplin, a local plumber's merchant (not the comedian), and out of the blue he offered to lend me his Rolls-Royce for the day. Well at first I was a little reluctant, thinking of the responsibility of getting it there and back in one piece. Happily, he wouldn't take no for an answer and what a moment it was when I pulled up outside Denise's house in the Rolls. There were one or two curtains twitching in the road that day. We had a fabulous time, and what's more, the car came back none the worse for having had me at the wheel.

It wasn't too often we got days out during the week because the new manager, Johnny Giles worked us hard. There were no complaints though. He was fair and won the respect of everybody. Having done well in my first three games, I was hoping to get more chances as the new season got underway. The new manager called us together when he first arrived and his message was clear and simple. His team would be picked on merit and merit alone. The players who proved themselves would be rewarded. It was a promise I held him to later, in my first real confrontation with a football manager. As the 1975–76 season got underway there was an encouraging mood of confidence in the dressing room. That took a dent in the first week, as Southampton beat us 3-0 and John Giles' first home game finished in a disappointing goal-less draw. My first chance came against Luton in the second week and thankfully we won 1-0. I was sub for the next couple of matches, and from then on it was a case of taking the chance when an injury or suspension to one of the other players meant changes. Soon there were only four more games before Christmas, but I was happy biding my time because I knew that sooner or later I would get the chance to stake a claim for a regular place.

Playing for John Giles was a great experience. His management gradually had effect after a shaky start. For the first few months we were near the bottom of the second division, and there were several papers and a few supporters ready to have a go. The manager appeared to have everything under control, although I think it was difficult for him at first, getting used to the role of player-manager. Off the field he was the boss, but as soon as he pulled his shirt on in the dressing room, he was one of us . . . a player. Every manager has different ideas about training and coaching and some of Giles' methods were unusual. I had always been used to the regimented ways of running, exercises, practising moves from free-kicks and corners, and working out defensive and attacking patterns. Under Giles, training was one big game of five-a-side. Nearly every morning training would be taken up with a five-a-side match. Most teams finish off training with a quick game which can often be a lighthearted affair, like the old players against the young ones, or defence against attack but there was nothing lighthearted about the Albion five-a-sides. They were fiercely competitive and played at a breathtaking rate. Slackness would not go unnoted and Giles demanded everything from his players. He invariably got it of course, and his training methods worked. The team gradually climbed the table and by New Year promotion talk was in the air.

The manager had strengthened the side by signing two fellow Irishmen. Mick Martin arrived from Manchester United and Paddy Mulligan blew in from Chelsea. Apart from their obvious skills on the field those two jokers boosted the dressing room morale no end. What a double act they were. Martin and Mulligan I'm sure would have done a bomb in music hall. Jokes and stories came flowing out, and no one was spared their ribbing or practical jokes. As one of the younger players I used to enjoy sitting in the dressing room and listening to their banter. Both were masters of sarcasm and anybody who dared to take them on would be easily cut down with words. Now and again they'd have a go at me for being quiet, and the secret was to sit there and take it. There was no way I was going to swallow the bait and have a go back at them! The good thing though about them was that they could also take jokes back. One of the most hilarious incidents came after training one morning. Mick Martin had turned up wearing a very natty pair of white shoes. In those days, white shoes in West Bromwich, even at a football club, were quite something. Mick had to take an awful lot of wisecracks when he walked in. Then after training, when he went to get changed another shock was in store for him. We all knew that the little Scottish winger Willie Johnston had done something to Mick's gleaming white shoes, but we weren't sure quite what. So, when Mick came to slip his shoes back on, everyone was staring at him. He struggled to get his foot inside and looked totally confused when neither shoe would move. Much to the delight of the dressing room the white shoes had been nailed to the floor. Not surprisingly that was the last we saw of them, but Mick more than got his own back over the weeks with his dazzling wit.

During the first few seasons at Albion I wore every number shirt except the goalkeeper's. And shortly after celebrating my nineteenth birthday I was back in the first team in the number nine shirt. The next match I wore six, then four and then three. Bryan Robson was usually the team change on the programme. Being an all-rounder, or utility player, had its advantages and disadvantages. On the plus side I was first reserve, so got a game when one of the senior players dropped out for one reason or another. On the other hand, I was dying to be given a real opportunity to play in midfield which has always been my favourite and strongest position.

That winter I had a run of eight games, the best yet, and Albion were really in the promotion chase. We pushed up from sixth to third and with just six games to go were neck and neck with Bolton and Bristol City with Sunderland out in front. In a home match against Blackpool I limped off with a strain and that was just about the end of my season.

For the final promotion push, Johnny Giles relied on experience and I was back on the bench as substitute. It was harder watching than playing with the chase for division one getting closer all the time. It went to the last match of the season. We were away to Oldham on the Saturday. A win would clinch promotion. The M6 motorway north that morning was thick with Albion supporters. As the team coach swept past, there were waves and car horns sounding out their support. It was like travelling to a Cup Final although our destination was a long way from Wembley. Oldham's Boundary Park ground was filled with 22,500 people and 15,000 of those were from the Midlands. 'Johnny Giles walks on water' was the chant thundering around the ground, and it was so loud it seeped into the dressing room where the manager's team talk was being delivered. It was short and wonderfully simple:

'If you want to play in the first division next season, if you want to go to Anfield, Old Trafford and Highbury again then today's your only chance.'

If Oldham beat us it would let in their Lancashire

neighbours Bolton. The Wanderers were playing at Charlton and I reckon there were a few hundred of their supporters at Boundary Park trying to help their cause by siding with Oldham. At half-time it was nil-nil. A real nail-biting match. Oldham had not had a good season but there was no way they were going to sit back and let Albion walk all over them. On top of that we were jittery and the tenseness of the occasion was showing. During the break Johnny Giles went round to every man, gently reassuring them the game could still be won. News that Bolton were 1-0 in their match rubbed salt into the wounds – the gap was closing and the pressure building up. The second half of the game began to go much the same as the first. Then after ten minutes the goal came. The ball was played down the right, the cross from Martin was headed down by Ally Brown to Tony 'Bomber' Brown. He swayed, juggled it from right to left foot and thumped it into the top corner of the net.

For the last thirty-five minutes Albion hung on and when the whistle finally went the pitch was awash with supporters. On the bench we jumped up and down and I can remember hearing the manager's team talk come flowing back into my mind as everybody made for the tunnel. Anfield, Old Trafford and Highbury would be on the visiting list next season, and of course, so would be St James Park, the home of my first football memories.

The champagne corks cracked against the ceiling as the celebrations got under way. I may have been sub but I'd done my bit and like everybody else the thought of promotion and the first division filled me with inspiration. What a season lay ahead – or so I thought.

# 5
## *Mixed Fortunes*

'The English first division is the best league in the world to play in' is a well-worn phrase, to be found in most football books and annuals. Well, hopefully I was going to find out for myself, as Albion prepared for the new season back in the first division. The team that started at Leeds for the first game was the one that had won promotion. My first chance came to play against the mighty Liverpool in a League Cup replay at the Hawthorns. The sight of those famous red shirts is enough to send a quiver of fear through anybody, Liverpool were reigning league champions and Kevin Keegan was at his best. They had scored in every game so far and I was pitched into battle because of an injury to Johnny Giles. In a memorable game we scraped home 1-0. To have played against the great Liverpool team was the biggest challenge for me so far, and to have won was a thrilling achievement. I had held my own against the best Britain had to offer.

The Liverpool game was on a Monday night and for the next few days I floated on air. My confidence had never been greater and I was eagerly awaiting Saturday's game – a local derby against Birmingham City at St Andrews. So imagine my disappointment when, on Friday lunchtime, John Giles pulled me aside and broke the news . . . I'd been relegated to substitute again. He was fit and wanted to play the tried and trusted eleven. Until then I had rarely raised a word in opposition against anybody. I had always been willing to learn and wait for the chance to claim a regular place. But now, for the first time, I felt hard done by. I listened to the manager, trying to hide the disappointment. Being dropped or left out of a team is the most disheartening feeling there is, especially when you think it's unjustified. You stand there and put on a brave face, while inside your stomach is churning over. Fortunately it is something of which I've not had too much experience.

One time that's always stuck in my mind came with England in Australia shortly before the European Championships in 1980. It was more an England 'B' team really and a couple of places in the squad for Italy were still open. I, along with Glen Hoddle, Gary Birtles, Peter Barnes and Laurie Cunningham were all hoping for a call. In Sydney we beat Australia 2-1, although I had to come off with cramp just before the end. I was pleased with what I had done, and when Ron Greenwood pulled me to one side at the airport, I thought a squad place was going to be mine. The news was bad. I hadn't made the England party for the European Championships. The manager had a completely logical reason for not choosing me and was full of praise and encouragement, but he was wasting his words. I felt lost and dejected and that long haul back from Australia was perhaps the worst journey I've ever had. My disappointment was such that I had nothing to say to Ron Greenwood and sat and felt sorry for myself. His mind was made up and I was too tired and flattened to argue.

But I argued with Johnny Giles when he left me out of the Albion team that first time. It was the first real confrontation I'd had with a manager. I knew I was no match with words, because Giles was perhaps one of the most eloquent and intelligent football managers you could come across. He had a bit of the Irish blarney, but he was no bullshitter that's for sure. I'd watched and listened before when some of the older players had complained or argued with him, and they were quickly outclassed and outwitted. Giles was as quick and clever off the field as he was on it. So what chance a nineteen-year-old?

'To be honest boss I don't think it's fair. I held my own against Liverpool and I think I deserve another chance. Others played worse than me.' I paused to study his reaction and waited for a reply. He frowned and nodded but said nothing, forcing me to go on. 'Well I've been in and out of the team for some time now and to be honest I reckon I should get more of a chance to show what I can do. You can't keep chopping and changing me around.'

Giles thought for a few moments and then came back at me.

'Well, I'm sorry how you feel about it Bryan, but I've got to put our strongest team out tomorrow, that's my job, and at the moment I think it's important we stay as we are. Next week I may well change my mind and bring you in again.'

With nothing left to say I went home, convincing myself on the way the manager was wrong and I should have been playing. The next morning we reported to a local hotel for a pre-match meal and meeting. The manager was in reception and when I walked in came straight over. I was worried that he was going to have a go at me for doubting his team selection, but in fact, quite the opposite happened.

'I've been giving what you said yesterday some thought Bryan, and have decided to play you in the middle. I'll be sub. I know you won't let me down.'

I must have thanked him ten times in as many seconds. There was nothing else I could think of to say. What a gesture . . . the player-manager dropping himself. Although you may think I am biased in saying what a fair man Giles was, it is that kind of action which puts some managers apart from others. There are those whose word is law and heaven help anybody who goes against it, while others are happy to listen to arguments and not be too big or proud to change their minds and admit they were wrong. I'm not saying Giles was wrong to drop me, but from that day on, my respect for him was unshakable. Happily we won that derby game against Birmingham City. A crowd of just under forty thousand made my first division debut quite a day. The ever reliable Bomber Brown got the winner and afterwards I was eager for more first division action. Although the manager returned for the next game I switched to left back and three matches later came the first of those fateful injuries. A first team place was really not in mind from then on. All I was worried about were my legs. But if ever there was a bitter sweet season then this was it.

There can't be many sportsmen who have suffered such a mixture of fortunes. Three broken legs in seven months, a call-up for the England under-21 team, a first ever hat-trick and my first appearance at Old Trafford. I had to withdraw from the England squad in March 1977 to play for Albion against Manchester United. At the time, I cursed my luck, but the roar of fifty-one thousand fans inside the ground soon changed my mind. A visit to Old Trafford, one of football's cathedrals, was a trip every player looked forward to. That season United were pushing for the championship. As you leave the dressing rooms and emerge from the tunnel at Old Trafford, it's like stepping straight from the cold silence of a doctor's waiting room to the rowdy, boisterous rhythm of a roaring party. The deafening noise overwhelms you and on my first visit there I spent the first few minutes before kick-off just gazing in awe at the packed stands. Although the vast majority are shouting you down in favour of their beloved reds, the atmosphere is unbelievable. There's no finer feeling than to play well in front of a big crowd and that first night at Old Trafford it hit me, for the first time, how grand it would be to play on this spectacular stage week in, week out.

To teams such as the Albion it was one of the best outings of the year. A 2-2 draw and a goal for me made it all the more enjoyable but Old Trafford, win or lose, is a place you hate leaving. The ground and Manchester United are like a disease – once into your bloodstream there is no escaping their charm and passion for good football. A few weeks before my first memorable game there, came the other highspot of the season. Ipswich, another side in the running for the championship, were at the Hawthorns and we felled them 4-0. It was one of those days when everything I did came off. Every pass found its man. Every tackle told and every shot was bang on target. The force must have been with me, and three chances finished as three goals – my first hat-trick. And as a prize I received the match ball and a host of headlines. The following morning I rushed down to the newsagent's and for the first time bought every paper I could lay my hands on. The young lady behind the counter looked rather puzzled as I piled them all up and then marched off out. All the match reports were carefully cut out and proudly dispatched back to Chester-le-Street. After the misery and pain of two broken legs, the hat-trick and the game at Old Trafford lifted my flagging confidence but of course there was another plateful of problems around the corner with the third broken leg against Manchester City.

The summer was long, hot and tiring. While everybody else disappeared to enjoy their holidays, I concentrated on getting fit. For much of the time I trained alone, gradually pushing myself harder and further. The new season brought a new manager to Albion. John Giles had returned to Ireland to run Shamrock Rovers as a managing director type figure. His ideas of managers having more say in clubs were a little too progressive, I think, for Albion directors and he had decided to seek his football utopia elsewhere. His place was taken by Ronnie Allen, who was no stranger to the place. To older fans he was still a treasured memory, the man whose cavalier goalscoring had won them the FA Cup over twenty years before. He had been chief scout under Giles and seemed to have a genuine appreciation of the game.

We started well and climbed to third spot with Everton and Forest, the eventual champions, just above us. I had taken over John Giles' role in midfield and was enjoying a settled run, thinking that the injury troubles and turbulence of the early days were over. But just before Christmas Ronnie Allen left. The lure of Saudi Arabia and their golden football riches took him away. Club captain John Wile took his place on a temporary basis and I was shocked to find myself amongst his early changes. A couple of defeats called for action and my midfield place disappeared. Although I was disappointed, I accepted the criticism that my game had fallen away a little. In the New Year yet another manager arrived. This time it was Ron Atkinson of the third division Cambridge United. He'd won acclaim for taking tiny United from the fourth division to the verge of the second in successive seasons. His record was an impressive one.

On first meeting Ron, I was struck by this friendly and lighthearted sort of chap. He was a man who enjoyed his football and liked others to share it with him. At the same time he was firm. He brought in Colin Addison, a renowned warrior with Forest and Arsenal and a successful manager with Hereford and Newport, as his assistant. The new manager was not one to make drastic changes though, and he stayed with the team he had inherited, which meant my chances were few and far between. Albion reached the FA Cup semi-final but went down to Ipswich 3-1. Getting so near and failing left the club deflated but injuries at least allowed me to show Ron Atkinson what I was capable of, and after the semi-final I was called in for the rest of the season.

I was now twenty-one, and for the first time began to wonder whether there was a better future for me away from West Bromwich Albion. I could not really count myself as a first-team regular and rumours about my future had unsettled me. Wolves and Aston Villa were reported to be interested in me and there was also the chance to go to America to play for Dallas. I was a bit fed up with life. At that age you feel capable of taking on the world and winning, but I honestly thought it was time to have a good hard think. I confronted Ron Atkinson, and he told me in no uncertain manner to forget leaving the club, and instead concentrate on playing for the Albion. We had won a place in Europe and with a summer tour of China on the horizon I decided to give it at least another year.

The historic trip to China was a landmark for all of us. Never before had a western football team travelled beyond the Great Wall of China. Most club tours took you to Europe or Scandinavia, so a trip to the Far East was an expedition into the unknown. Having read and heard stories of Communist China, Mao Tse Tung and the Cultural Revolution, none of us was quite sure what to expect. The club had stressed to us how we were going as ambassadors for British sport in general, and it was important we made the right impression. China was certainly different. It made me realize how lucky we are in this country. One trip took us to a commune in the countryside. The people were out working in the fields while the children packed into the local schoolhouse. It was the living quarters which took us by surprise. We had to duck to get in through the low narrow doorway and inside it was so basic. Table and chairs and wooden beds with no real signs of what we would associate with comfort. The people, though, were so friendly and bright, and I admired the way they tackled their lives. The burning desire to learn was the thing that struck me most as they made their homes and country open to us. There were plenty of sightseeing trips and one memorable journey took us to the Great Wall. Now, as a kid I can remember being taken to Hadrian's Wall which was not far from home. Such a long wall used to puzzle me as a child, but faced with the Great Wall of China I was breathless. It travelled for miles over hills and through valleys and you couldn't but wonder how it was ever built. Team mate John Trewick was beside me as I gazed towards the horizon and what was his reaction to one of the wonders of the world?

'When you've seen one wall, you've seen them all!' chirped John. It's just as well the Chinese interpreter was out of earshot!

We were in China to play football of course, but the people loved to welcome us to their cities. Everywhere we went there were receptions and banquets and I wondered one evening whether we were being cleverly sabotaged. On the eve of a major game in Peking against the national team we were all invited to a splendidly colourful banquet at the local hall. I was always brought up to clear my plate whenever I was out and old habits die hard. Tray after tray of exotic food was brought in and served, a little at a time. At first I cleared my plate with ease, each time thinking I'd about had enough. But the quicker you ate the faster the next delicacy was dished up. After twelve courses I lost count, and started to wonder when it was going to finish. At this rate, I thought, the Chinese will slay us tomorrow, because none of us will be able to move! Still the food kept coming and we were all too polite to turn it away. I've never been more pleased to hear after dinner speeches as I sat there feeling as though I'd been blown up with a pump.

The next day we looked far better than we felt, but a crowd of around eighty-thousand wildly enthusiastic fans at the national stadium brought us all to life. It did not take long to run all the rice and chop suey off as the Chinese darted in and out.

The Chinese are great competitors and we were content to beat them 2-1. I have a feeling though, that the next time we see a football team from China they will surprise many with their speed and skill. The trip to China was a great experience and it had done a great deal for Albion. Apart from the prestige from such a demanding and sensitive tour, we came back a welded unit under an ambitious manager ready for the challenge of European football.

Atkinson and Addison were a fine partnership. They were a delight to work for. Football, training and life in general was fun and the players responded to their friendly and open approach. During the coming season, Albion were to celebrate their centenary and it was by far the most enjoyable time at the club. European travels took us to Turkey, Portugal, Spain and Yugoslavia and just after Christmas we went to the top of the first division.

That Albion team was the finest I played in at the

Hawthorns. It had a wonderful blend and one can only speculate at what could have been achieved if it stayed together. Tony Godden in goal was perhaps one of the most underrated players in the first division. Full-backs Brendan Batson and Derek Statham could not only defend, but open up opposing defences with their enterprising runs down the wing. Skipper John Wile and Alistair Robertson were unshakable in defence. In midfield there was Len Cantello, a strong and yet intricate ball player who ran many a match; Tony Brown, unstoppable on his day and myself. 'The Black Flash', Laurie Cunningham played wide. He had it all; his flying speed and dazzling ball control made him amongst the best in the world. And finally, up front was Cyrille Regis, a commanding centre-forward who has far more ability than many give him credit for and alongside him Ally Brown, whose finishing was devastating. What a team that was! We reached the quarter finals of the UEFA Cup, made it to the fifth round of the FA cup and finished third in the table. We actually went to the top at one stage, but over Christmas and the New Year the snow and ice took its grip and there was one postponement after another. All our good football was played before the bad weather set in. Weeks of sitting waiting for the thaw seemed to affect us and we never really recaptured our early form. I am still convinced that, if it had not been for the terrible weather that year, Albion would have won one of the major competitions.

The team's success brought me an international call to the England under-21 side – at the age of twenty-two! I was one of the over-age players named in the squad to face Wales at Swansea. On an icy cold February night, wearing the number nine shirt I made my debut. Only 5,500 fans braved the snow to watch the game, which was a long way from being a classic. The only good thing about it was the result. We won 1-0 with Glen Hoddle getting the goal.

At the end of the season came the greatest match of my life: on June 2 1979 Denise and I were married at Wesley Church in West Bromwich. What a rush it all was. The week before Albion had been on an end of season tour to Denmark. We returned home on the Friday and the next day we were married, and then after just one night of wedded bliss, I waved goodbye to Denise to join the England under-21 squad. So a real honeymoon had to wait for a few weeks. Denise, as always, was wonderful about it. Losing your husband on a football tour after just one day can't be easy, but she never complained.

Although I was looking forward to touring with the England squad, the company of seventeen footballers is hardly the ideal way to start married life. But off I went, and it turned out to be quite a trip. At the end of the under-21 matches I was lucky enough to be selected for a 'B' international. England travelled to Klagenfurt to play the Austrian 'B' team and this match will go down in football history. It was the middle of June and in the morning we had enjoyed the warmth and sun. The first half was a belter. I cracked in a thundering shot from twenty-five yards (23 metres) to give us a goal lead and at half-time we trooped into the dressing room sweating our socks off. But then after half-time the skies began to close up and darken. The air got heavy and humid and all of a sudden a crack of lightning rattled around the outside of the stadium. Hailstones as big and hard as marbles came pelting down. The referee rushed us off to the dressing room and the fans rushed for cover. For ten minutes or so it rattled down and when the storm cleared the pitch was unplayable. Imagine my difficulty in trying to tell Denise that a freak hailstorm had finished off my debut for the England 'B' team. She reckoned I was receiving my come-uppance for leaving a bride at home with her mum! Happily, on a real honeymoon in Ibiza there wasn't a hailstorm in sight.

# 6
# *The England Call*

As the eighties dawned, an exciting new breakthrough was on the horizon – the chance to play for England. Youth, under-21 and 'B' internationals are all good experience, but any footballer will tell you that they are no substitute for the real thing.

Whatever the sport, to represent your country is one of the greatest goals anyone can achieve in life. From the very first day of kicking a football any young lad dreams of playing for England at Wembley, or Scotland at Hampden. There's that old story from the Welsh valleys of lads pulling on the red Welsh shirt and becoming men. Well it might all sound a little romantic but to me and many other footballers who have been fortunate enough to play at international level, the first game for your country is like coming of age. It's the passing out parade for the chosen few. International football brings a whole new adventure. The chance to play against the best in the world, at the very peak of your sport. Life changes, because more is expected of you, and everybody looks to an England player. You can't afford to make too many mistakes, because nothing goes unnoticed. The supporters, managers, press and even other players watch you closer, and reputation of course counts for very little on a football field. It can be more of a burden and some players have suffered from their own success, feeling that they always have to play better and better. It's natural for supporters to expect more and more but the result can be players cracking under the strain.

From my first international to this day I like to think I give my all – whether it's for club or country. Sometimes it's not enough to save your side from a disappointing result, what you have to do is soldier on regardless. Pressure, strain and worry make good headlines in papers and half the time I'm convinced players suffer by reading or hearing about them. They are all self-inflicted but there's no doubt the international player can be more susceptible to them. International football brings many rewards, but it can also prove a hurdle that many stumble at. When you look through the record books there are many players who've made no more than a handful of appearances for their country. Some are unlucky, perhaps overshadowed by better players, such as the other goalkeepers when Banks was at his best, or the many wingers waiting behind Matthews. But an awful lot were given the chance and many failed to cope with the step up. So playing for your country can really make or break you. There are those that fall by the wayside and content themselves with league football, while others thrive on a wealth of experience. An international call-up is the watershed of any player's career and mine could not have come in a stranger way. I don't worry much or suffer from strain and it's just as well really when you consider how my first chance came.

As a regular member of the under-21 team I was hoping to be given the chance of promotion to the senior squad. My form with Albion was good but it was Glen Hoddle of Spurs who seemed to be in favour. With Kevin Keegan, Trevor Brooking and Terry McDermott all there as well, there were not many openings in the team and I wondered whether my chance would disappear. But the power of the press worked in my favour this time and came to the rescue. My performances for Albion had gone down well in the Midlands but there is always the feeling that players with the more glamorous clubs such as Liverpool, Manchester United and Arsenal are more likely to catch the eye. I think it's inevitable they do, but at the same time an England manager rarely overlooks a good player, no matter which club he plays for.

In the days running up to the selection of a team or squad there would be speculation about who Ron Greenwood, the manager, would choose. My name was consistently mentioned but every time it was missing. Reporters would ask me what I thought of being overlooked and supporters would come up to me in the streets and moan about the England selection. All I could do was shrug my shoulders, although inside I was wondering whether my chance would ever come. Well, one evening the *Birmingham Mail* launched an amazing campaign. Their object was to get Bryan Robson in the England team. Now I didn't know anything about it until I read the paper that night! It said I had been unfairly overlooked by England manager Ron Greenwood, and deserved a chance. The paper felt that, because Albion was not one of the most famous clubs, and the Midlands wrongly thought of as a backwater, I was being ignored. They pointed out that I was twenty-three and reckoned to be one of the most consistent players in the first division. It was flattering to have such a campaign launched, and over the next couple of weeks it really got up steam. So many local people wrote and phoned in to the paper that a special form was printed on the back page. Readers were invited to complete the form which said that I should be in the England team and send it in. The local paper apparently were snowed under with forms. Over a thousand people wrote in and the paper pointed out that it was one of the biggest responses they'd ever had. The paper's chief soccer reporter, Ray Matts, who's now moved on to the *Daily Mail*, had the task of sending all the forms down to FA headquarters in Lancaster Gate for the England manager to see for himself.

The paper went out of its way to point out to Mr Greenwood that it was not trying to tell him his job, but wanted to give him some idea of just how strongly the local people felt. The England manager, I think, was a little annoyed at being put on the spot by the paper and accused of not picking the right men. He assured me through the club though, and the local paper, that I was not being overlooked for any sinister reason. My chance would come, he said, if I maintained my form. Well, whether it was my form or that marvellous poll which finally convinced Ron Greenwood I was worth an England place I'm not sure but on February 6 1980 my chance came at last when I played at Wembley against the Republic of Ireland. Apart from being my first International, it was my first appearance at the stadium, so there was a double challenge that evening.

When you ask players about Wembley matches, whether it be for England or in a Cup Final, they will often say it passes them by. They are so wrapped up in the game that the occasion is forgotten. The only thing that sticks in my mind about that first game for England is emerging from that vast, cold tunnel to the echoing roar of thousands of people. The whole stadium spreads out before you and I just gazed around in awe, not fully realizing I was achieving the ambition that burns in any footballer. The game was not a great one, we won 2-0 with Kevin Keegan scoring both goals and I suppose I was satisfied with my night's work. It was not one of my best games but I think I proved a point and justified not only Ron Greenwood's decision to select me but also the backing of all those Midlanders and their 'Robson for England' campaign.

The campaign had made me feel a little awkward with the England manager at first. I wondered how hurt he'd been by the petition. My anxiety of having upset Mr Greenwood was not called for. He only mentioned the campaign in passing during a brief chat in training and more than made me welcome. As a manager I found Ron Greenwood extremely fair and very competent. The England job must be a thankless task. Success brings you all the friends and allies you could ever wish for – while anything short of the best makes you the most beleaguered man in football.

I'm sure many managers have longed to be given the chance to run the national team and yet those who have had the chance must have had the same longing to give it up. What many forget is that a league manager is judged over forty-two league matches and half a dozen or so cup games each season while the England manager has only around a dozen matches a year in which to mould his team and achieve the heights. Two or three defeats for a national team hit hard and create problems. On the whole I thought Ron Greenwood coped very well. There was immense respect for him throughout the game and he was a popular figure with the players. No one doubted his craft as a coach and tactician and I always admired him for the way he conducted his duties.

Mr Greenwood is a gentleman who carried out his role with great presence and dignity. The only characteristic I could never come to terms with was the way he kept his emotions very much to himself. Obviously he shared the joy of a win and would mourn defeat but for a lot of the time I felt he kept a lot of his feelings back from the players. That can be a help because a manager who panics and worries can easily unsettle his team but there were times with England when Ron was perhaps a little too silent. Every manager has his own style. The colourful men such as Atkinson, Allison, Docherty and Bond are contrasted by the quieter figures of Sexton, Paisley and Saunders. Mr Greenwood fell somewhere in the middle. I can remember studying him once during an after match inquest and the conclusion I drew was that he was retaining some of his stronger feelings. I like people to speak their minds, and I suppose being blunt and to the point is more of a northern trait. Ron Greenwood, I reckon, should not have kept so much inside him. Instead he should have let off steam more often and that may well have eased the burden of his onerous task.

I remember walking back to the dressing room in Oslo in September 1981 when England had just been humiliated by Norway in a World Cup qualifier. We had lost a vital game 2-1 and our chances of making it to the finals in Spain seemed to have gone. Nobody had to tell us what a poor result it was but many managers would have locked the dressing room door and ripped us apart. Ron Greenwood was obviously shaken by the setback and went back over some of the mistakes and misses we'd made. There were no raised voices or violent arguments and he was his usual restrained self. I think he was holding back and there was far more anger and disappointment inside him than any of us realized. He was quieter than usual on the journey home and watching him at the airport and on the plane I felt sorry that one man was having to carry the can for the mistakes of so many others. If I had been the manager in that dressing room in Oslo, I would have given every player a good slating and got everything off my chest. Ron Greenwood was different. He was a hard man to read but, even though he failed to let his real emotions out, he still did a good job for England. I may have cursed him when he left me out of the European Championship squad in the summer of 1980 but that was me being selfish. After the disappointment of those championships my chance came, and I thoroughly enjoyed playing under Ron Greenwood.

In footballing terms, playing for England really opens your eyes. You play against a wider variety of teams and the chance to mix with other players is a great education. I know that in the past club managers feared the players comparing wages and contracts with each other, ending up with somebody realizing he wasn't being paid his worth and going back home and demanding more money or a transfer. Those times have changed because by and large international players are all fairly paid and I've never heard players speak about the money they earn. Some obviously earn more than others but with incentive schemes now widely in use the maxim is basically that success brings its just rewards.

Playing for England did not make me starry eyed but it made me realize that perhaps the future could be brighter away from West Bromwich Albion. In the 1979–80 season, the club managed to finish tenth after a desperately poor start. We were bottom at one stage and dispatched from the UEFA cup by the East German team Carl Zeiss Jena in the first round. Fortunately our form picked up with the New Year but it wasn't the season we had envisaged, especially with new signings such as winger Peter Barnes and midfielder Gary Owen in the team.

The next season was much better and in the first few weeks I found I had plenty on my mind. Denise was expecting our first child and the baby was due in September. The first few months of a new season are always hectic and Denise was worried the baby would come on a

Saturday afternoon, or on a night when I was playing. Strangely, in the first week we didn't have a night match our daughter Claire was born, and for me, it was one of the most nerve-racking and yet fulfilling moments of my life.

It was 2 A.M. on Wednesday, September 17 1980, when Denise woke me to say the pains had started. There had been one or two false alarms so we decided to wait for a few hours to see how things went. The pains increased and so after a few pots of tea and a call to the hospital we decided it was time to go. But not before one of the most bizarre incidents I can recall. People always joke about nervous fathers pacing up and down outside hospital wards waiting for the first cries of a new baby. I didn't think I was nervous, but as Denise got her case ready to go to hospital, I announced I was going upstairs to do some painting. Do-it-yourself has never been my strong point and I can't ever recall doing any painting, in or around the house, so you can imagine Denise's look of utter bewilderment as I disappeared upstairs to do some painting. I don't know what came over me, just losing my head like that. When I got to the top of the stairs it suddenly dawned on me, what on earth was I going to paint – and come to that where was I going to get a brush and tin of paint from? Denise was calling me from downstairs and then I came to my senses and away we went to the hospital. We still laugh about that morning because as Denise says that's the one and only time I've ever offered to do some decorating. It must have been nerves, and it's just as well that Denise didn't tell the doctor what sort of state I was in because if she had he would never have let me watch at the birth.

Watching Claire being born was one of the most moving experiences of my life. A new person suddenly emerging and bursting into being; that day changed me in many ways. It taught me to appreciate the everyday things that we all take for granted, like health and happiness, and it also made me more responsible. Looking down on our red, wrinkled baby daughter, swathed in white, I realized that we now had much more to care for than just ourselves.

Back on the football field some of the old style was returning to Albion. Under Ron Atkinson and his new assistant Mick Brown the team settled down well and we finally finished up fourth in the table, made it to the fifth round of the League Cup and won a place in Europe. But as the season finished and I made off with the England squad for vital World Cup matches against Switzerland and then Hungary times were changing at the Hawthorns. Manchester United, having parted company with their manager Dave Sexton, were chasing a big name replacement. Bobby Robson, who was then in charge of Ipswich and Southampton's Laurie McMenemy were the two front-runners. Both decided they were better staying where they were, so the search went on. In the end United turned towards Ron Atkinson of the Albion. I don't know why they hadn't thought of him sooner. He had a good grounding in the game and his work with West Bromwich had been impressive. Perhaps, more important, he had style and when it came down to it, United wanted a manager with a character befitting one of the most famous and colourful clubs in the world. So in a blaze of headlines, Ron Atkinson was offered and accepted the job at Old Trafford. It wasn't quite as simple as that, because Albion refused to let him go and insisted that a new contract keeping him at the Hawthorns had been agreed upon even though it was not signed. I found myself in a strange position because the Albion chairman was Mr

Bert Millichip, who was also a senior figure within the Football Association. He was shortly to become its chairman and was with us on the England tour.

It was difficult for me to concentrate on England when the whole future of the Albion manager, and therefore to a great extent the club, was being aired around in the background. As usual there were so many stories that you were not quite sure which to believe and I was dying to get hold of Mr Millichip and ask him what was really going on. But I knew my place as a player and realized it was not for the likes of me to go barging into talks between chairman and manager. Finally Ron Atkinson went off to Manchester United, with Albion breathing fire about an agreement which they thought had been broken. Relations between the two clubs were a little cold and as I went on holiday with Denise and Claire I could hardly have expected what was coming next.

# 7
## *Changes at the Albion*

If you flick through any football record book the name of West Bromwich Albion will always be there. 'The Baggies' have enjoyed their lives with five FA Cup wins and one league championship. Illustrious names such as Bobby Robson, Don Howe, Derek Kevan and Jeff Astle have passed through and the club has always commanded respect. The supporters may not challenge those of Liverpool in number but the Albion fans are a good bunch. They know their football and always respond to success. Sadly though, with Albion there is a feeling of second best about it. I don't mean that in any disrespectful way but if you sat down and named the top ten English clubs, would West Bromwich Albion come on your list? I had joined the Albion as a schoolboy because the club impressed me. They were more caring than many others, and from top to bottom it was well organized. My seasons at the Hawthorns had been happy ones, but life is so desperately short for a footballer and I make no secret of my ambitions. Playing for England was one, but there was so much more to go for. League championships, FA Cups, League Cups – European Cups. The list is a long and challenging one.

The departure of Ron Atkinson threw doubt over my own future as the club were offering me a new contract. I was already signed up, but they wanted me to extend the contract for six years and also to improve the terms. Money has never been my main incentive in life. Like all of us I enjoy some of the luxuries it can bring and footballers have to make the most of their careers in a financial sense. But I have never put riches before happiness and contentment. I knew Albion were willing to make me a lucrative new deal to persuade me to invest my future with them. It called for plenty of thought and my final decision to leave had nothing to do with contracts or fabulous signing-on fees. It was ambition that took me.

The Albion team were a good bunch of men. There were the promising players like Gary Owen, Peter Barnes, Cyrille Regis and Derek Statham and then the dependables, club captain John Wile and his defensive partners Ally Robertson and Brendan Batson. The club's record goalscorer Tony Brown was still around along with his namesake Ally Brown, another chap who could always be relied upon to knock in the goals when they were wanted. The last two seasons at Albion were a bit of an anti-climax. The success the team was capable of had not been earned and there was a feeling in the club of being also-rans. We were always being pushed out in the final run-ins for trophies and you looked at the club and wondered whether it was prepared to really challenge the best. I used to sit and look around the dressing room at times. John Wile was an immensely likeable and intelligent man. As a centre-half he was among the most capable on his day as was the Scot Ally Robertson, who I roomed with on club trips. Then there was Tony 'Bomber' Brown, another fabulous professional, whose scoring record put him amongst the cream of the goal grabbers.

John Wile and 'Bomber' Brown had devoted their careers to Albion and I asked myself what had they won? 'Bomber's' moment of glory had come in 1968 when the 'Baggies' took the FA Cup with a win over Everton. But John Wile had won nothing with Albion except an awful lot of respect and friends. He had led the team to semi-finals, to championship chases, but every time they had lost out. In looking at these two in particular, I began to wonder whether if I stayed my career would go the way of theirs? I felt sorry and still do for men like these, they give so much to the game, and yet in the way of glory get so little back. I was determined that given the chance, I wanted to play at Wembley in a Cup Final, I wanted to play in a European Cup Final and enjoy it and so much more. I may never achieve all my ambitions but I'll always try and never want to look back and say to myself 'if only I'd done that or had a go at that . . .'

The departure of Ron Atkinson really spurred me on to leave. People accused him of walking out on Albion, but how could he turn down one of the most glamorous and challenging football jobs in the world? But my immediate future depended on who took over at the Hawthorns. With Ron Atkinson went his number two Mick Brown and reserve coach Brian Whitehouse, so it was a clean sweep. The papers were full of speculation. Alan Mullery's name was high on the list and there was also mention of John Giles returning, but in the end the job went to Ronnie Allen, who ironically had held the job before Ron Atkinson. Allen had been drawn by a big cash offer to Saudi Arabia and after that had travelled to work in Greece and Portugal.

The return of Ronnie Allen was welcomed by the supporters, many of whom still held fond memories of him leading the Albion attack of the fifties. His goals had helped win the FA Cup for the 'Baggies' in 1954 and on the outside he was a warm, witty and charming man. His reappointment hardly caused a ripple in the dressing room. There was one faction which sat back and thought better the devil you know, while others were disappointed the Board had not gone for a more imaginative appointment.

With Albion making such a song and dance about Manchester United allegedly poaching Ron Atkinson, it would have been hypocritical for them to do the same to another club. So basically, a lot of players felt the directors had picked a man who was readily available and that was Ronnie Allen.

When he was previously in charge it had been my comeback season after the broken legs and I was a young player making my way up. Then he was always helpful and considerate and we usually got on pretty well. One of his first tasks was to try to persuade me to sign a new contract. Rumours were already spreading that I wanted to leave, but they were premature. I was happy to talk to the new manager and hear what his plans were, both for me and the team.

Several other players were queuing up to see him as their contracts had come to an end, so the manager was in for a busy time. Our first meeting was friendly and informative. You can't help but be impressed on first meeting Ronnie Allen. For a man in his early fifties he still looks remarkably good. There is always a twinkle in his eye and his year-round tan and well-groomed greying hair make him look more like a business executive than a football manager. Ronnie Allen is a born optimist. He's a chap who rarely accepts failure and the morning we met he was his usual buoyant self. After the pleasantries had been exchanged the small, slim man leant back in his chair and spelled out his plans.

'I don't think the club has achieved its best in the last two seasons. If you look at the players we've got here we should be winning championships and making it to Cup Finals – not falling down with the finishing post in sight. I want the best, Bryan, and that means lads like you, along with some of the players we've got here and one or two others I've got my eye on. This club has an awful lot going for it.'

The remarks were those of all football managers in pre-season, as they set about the task of preparing their side for another season. Although my present contract was still in force he outlined how much more the club would be prepared to offer me to stay longer.

'Well to be honest boss, although money is important I'm also concerned about the future of the club. What sort of team are you going to get?' was my first reaction.

He leant back even further in his chair, pushed his hands together as though seeking some sort of divine guidance and came out with a blockbuster.

'Trevor Francis is one man I'm hoping to bring here. There's still a lot to be sorted out, but I reckon we can get him here to the Hawthorns.'

Trevor, the country's first one million pound footballer, was recovering from injury with Nottingham Forest and his future with them had been in doubt for some time. If Albion were in for Trevor Francis, I thought, then perhaps, the future at the Hawthorns would be quite something. Ronnie Allen and I agreed to leave things as they were and have another talk in a few days' time. But imagine my disappointment when I discovered from other players that despite the manager's optimism they had not signed, or agreed new contracts. On top of that I discovered Trevor Francis had not even heard that Albion was interested in signing him, nor was he expecting a call. Well, that heralded the start of one of the worst months of my career. The papers, by now, were full of stories about my future and of other clubs ready to break the transfer record to sign me.

After another talk with the manager when I challenged him about the so called Trevor Francis transfer, which he managed to wriggle around, I hinted I was thinking of asking for a transfer. He told me there and then that the club wouldn't consider letting me go and I should be sensible and accept the new contract.

We were busy preparing for a new season and there was friction in the dressing room. I wasn't the only player at odds with the manager and for the first time the Albion team was not a happy one. There was a current of discontentment running all the way through. The skipper John Wile had a lot on his plate, having taken on the extra responsibilities of coach and the problems of contracts and terms were gnawing away at team spirit. The pot was stirred by Remi Moses, one of my midfield partners, leaving to join forces again with Ron Atkinson at Manchester United, and you could not escape rumours that I was next for Old Trafford. Albion chairman Bert Millichip was adamant though. I was staying and the manager told the press: 'Robson leaves this club over my dead body!'

However, by this time I had discovered that Ronnie Allen either changed his mind and views about matters remarkably quickly or was even more of an optimist than anyone gave him credit for. In short, Ronnie Allen became a difficult man to deal with.

So the season started under a cloud. The Albion fans, naturally enough, were upset at what was going on. A section of the crowd thought I was betraying them by wanting to leave. I can understand how they felt, but did they realize how I felt? All the unsettling talks with the manager had left me frustrated and at that time the future looked brighter away from the Hawthorns. Finally Ronnie Allen came up with another offer. A new contract that would keep me with Albion for another six years, until I was thirty. The offer, of £1,000 a week, was a fabulous one by any standards and the promise of further incentives, plus rises, Albion had been more than generous. I took the offer home and told the manager I would sleep on it and give him an answer in the morning. That night Denise and I sat and talked it out. She was happy to stay, or willing to move if necessary. The money was good, but as we talked Denise really found the answer.

'These last few weeks, you haven't been the same. I can see you've not been enjoying it as much, and it's no good saying yes to this new offer if your heart's not in it,' she said.

Denise was right, my heart was not in it. I felt a move to a bigger club would give me the chances I was looking for. My mind was made up; in the morning I would ask for a transfer.

As I rushed downstairs in the morning, I felt freer than I had done for weeks. The new contract had been at the back of my thoughts all the time and no matter how hard I tried to get on with something else, I couldn't escape the future. But that morning I was bright and breezy. Until, that is, I picked up the paper. As I flicked to the back page there was a headline that burned into me: 'Albion's £1,000 a week offer to Robson'. The paper was running a story that Albion was preparing, for the first time in its history, to dig deep to try to persuade me to stay with them. It was all there, the offer had been made yesterday afternoon by Ronnie Allen, and it was the final one. I was angry, not at the paper, but at the club, who obviously had leaked the story. Skipping breakfast, I drove to the local newsagent's and bought a copy of every newspaper. They all had practically the same story and headline. So off I stormed to the ground to confront Ronnie Allen. Striding into his office, I threw the papers on his desk and demanded an explanation.

'I'm as angry as you, Bryan. Haven't a clue where it's come from. It's not me,' he said.

'Well, I want an explanation, my contract is private and the club's got no right to go telling anybody else. If it's not you, then somebody else must have said something. Anyway,' I said, charging on just as the manager was ready to come back at me, 'I've decided I don't want a new contract. I want to leave.'

That was it, the manager asked me to put the request in writing, and it would go before the board. But I didn't let those paper headlines go. After training I went home and started to phone around the local press lads. I knew that someone had leaked the details of my new contract and after a little bit of gentle persuasion I discovered it was one of the directors.

From then on I was determined to ve Albion. The transfer request was turned down by the board, but I told them I would not be happy staying – whatever the terms. My relationship with the manager deteriorated and my feelings about Albion and its lack of ambition were best summed up by a scene in the dressing room in Switzerland as we were preparing to play Zurich Grasshoppers in the first leg of a UEFA Cup match. On paper, it was a fairly even match and we were confident of making it to the second round. Imagine my astonishment then, when Ronnie Allen announced at the team talk that he would settle for a 1-0 defeat. There were thirty minutes to go and you could hear the rumblings of the crowd outside. A few hundred Albion supporters had made the trip and it was encouraging to hear their chants out there. It was an important match for us, but the manager was talking of defeat. Never before, or since, have I heard a manager dish out such a bewildering battle command. Most would be building us up, hammering home how well we would have to play. You may be underdogs at times, but when you're sitting in the dressing room waiting for the kick-off defeat is unthinkable.

'Remember lads, we've a second leg, a chance to get them back home and I'll settle for a 1-0 defeat. We can kill them at the Hawthorns' were the words with which Ronnie Allen was sending his team out. I glanced around at the rest of the lads and they all looked suitably unimpressed and some must have been flattened by the team talk.

It only went to prove that Albion lacked the killer instinct. Second best would do. We were beaten before we started – but the manager had no grounds for complaints afterwards. We got the result we wanted, a 1-0 defeat. Sadly we lost the second leg as well and that was the end of Europe and for me the end of Albion – the very next day I was on the move.

But the run up to the transfer was not that straightforward. When I asked for a move, I had three English clubs in mind, Arsenal, Liverpool and Manchester United and, if need be, I would consider a move abroad as a last resort. Albion finally agreed to let me go after weeks of arguments. At first when I turned down their new contract and asked for a move, they refused my request and insisted that I serve out the remaining two years of my existing contract. But I think after a time it dawned on them that it would be silly to keep an unhappy player and the money they would get for me would help buy fresh players for the club and perhaps swell the funds as well.

When Albion finally decided to listen to offers, Manchester United came in with a staggering bid of £1.5 million. Much to my astonishment Albion turned it down. They wanted £2 million!

I tried my best to keep up with what was going on by

calling in to see Ronnie Allen most days, either before, or after training. He kept me pretty well in the picture but some days I had to resort to reading the papers and watching the television news to learn exactly what was happening. It was crazy. My whole future as a footballer and the future of my family was in question and I was the last to know what was happening. Reporters would ring me at home and stop me at the club hoping for some news of what was building up to be the biggest transfer ever in the history of English soccer. I could tell them nothing, and more often they could tell me things.

The first time I knew that a transfer was finally going through was after the second leg of that UEFA Cup game with Zurich. Next morning there was no training but the manager asked me to go and see him and be ready for a move; Albion it appeared, had accepted a £1.8 million bid from Manchester United.

# 8
## *Transfer*

The day I signed for Manchester United was the easiest ninety minutes I'll ever have at Old Trafford. That's how long it took to complete the £1.8 million transfer, which not only made British football history, but was also to change my life.

It was Thursday, October 1 1981 when United and Albion finally agreed on a deal. The night before I'd played at my last game for Albion against Zurich Grasshoppers. We lost 3-1 in the home leg of our UEFA cup match and after the game manager Ronnie Allen hinted that the transfer would finally be going through. The next morning the call came. It was the news I'd been waiting weeks for, and the excitement in me started to build as Allen told me on the phone that everything had been settled between the two clubs and it was now up to me. Before leaving Manchester, I had to call in at the Hawthorns to pick up some papers and say a few goodbyes. Although I still had to agree on a contract with Manchester United, I knew deep down, that I was on my way to Old Trafford to sign, come what may.

There was a small gathering of press men at the ground when I got there and they all wanted to know the news. I was dying to tell them all, but now the deal was so close I daren't say anything silly, or assume too much. They knew, of course, that the clubs had agreed on a fee and I tried my hardest to curb my enthusiasm.

'Yes, I am going to meet Manchester United, and yes the clubs have settled on a fee but I'm not sure exactly how much money's involved and I've still got to meet United and sort out a contract,' I told them.

Despite the fact the last few months at the Hawthorns had been tinged with bitterness, I was saddened to be driving away. As a club they had looked after me well and all in all, I'd had some good times there. The supporters had always been friendly and by and large the atmosphere in the dressing room was good. I was excited at the prospect of moving to a club such as Manchester United but as I drove past the Albion ground for the last time a feeling of fear began to well in my stomach. It was something that one of the Albion lads, Andy King had said to me a few days earlier.

'We all respect you here Bryan and you've got nothing to prove. When you get to another club you'll have to win your respect again and show them you mean business,' was the friendly warning he'd given me. And that was worrying. At West Bromwich I was safe. I knew the club, the players and the officials inside out and I was well established in the team. Moving away meant fresh surroundings, strange faces and different ways. Many players stay with one club because they welcome the security the familiarity brings and fear the challenge of moving. There have been many players who've left one team as a top goalscorer or unbeatable defender, only to find themselves lost in a wilderness and unable to cope at their new club. Some go back while others struggle on, trying to rediscover their lost form.

At Albion, the club had broken their transfer record by paying just over half a million pounds for David Mills from Middlesbrough. At Ayresome Park he was the hero, and he came to West Bromwich with a well-earned reputation. Sadly, Dave never did settle, with injuries and bad luck hampering his career. It was thinking of people like him which made me a little apprehensive as we drove out of the town and headed north for Manchester.

As well as Denise, I drove up with my accountant Tony Price, who was along to advise me about the financial side of the deal. Some managers, I know, don't like players having accountants or agents. They fear the players may be manipulated too easily and the feeling is that agents try to squeeze too much money out of the game. But with a footballer, contracts can be complicated and there's a lot at stake when you're signing away five or six years, which in this game can be half of your career. There are some players who willingly accept a long-term offer, only to find themselves complaining about the contract a year or two later. By then of course, it's too late. Others try to sort things out on their own but these days there are so many pension schemes, insurance policies and other financial aspects to take into account, that if you're not careful you can lose yourself. Lack of knowledge can land you in trouble in later years, so that's why I took Tony along. In the car going up we discussed the move and I told Tony the sort of wage I was looking for. It was more a question of 'dotting the i's and crossing the t's', because we both knew that, barring any major mishap, I was going to sign for Manchester United.

As Old Trafford got closer I became more excited. Denise was fairly quiet. We'd talked for a long time about moving and the transfer was a big day for her as well. She'd lived in Birmingham all her life. Her family and friends were there and she too was a little nervous about moving away for the first time. She was happy to go though, because my unrest at Albion had rebounded on her at home. She knew that I'd been unsettled, and we'd agreed that a transfer was the only answer. Life would change for her as well. Apart from moving home, there would be increased pressure on her. The transfer was going to make me a personality, at least in the Manchester area, where anything to do with United was news. Albion had been one of football's quieter backwaters but now we were heading for the main stream, and the most famous football city in England.

The wave of interest hit us as soon as we drove into the ground. I'd only arrived before on a match day, in a team coach, with thousands of people making their way in. There were always big crowds there and even when there's no game people are drawn to Old Trafford. Kids hang around waiting for autographs and there's always a buzz of activity in and around the ground. As we pulled in the autograph hunters were there in force and so too were the press. News of the deal had travelled fast and as soon as I got out of the car the questions came flying in. Would I be signing today? Would I be playing for United on Saturday? What did it feel like to be the country's most expensive footballer? That last question, I knew would be thrown at me from every angle, but I managed to dodge most of the questions because now I was anxious to get inside rather than stand on the doorstep and speculate about what was going to happen.

When you step inside Old Trafford it's more like arriving at a swish hotel than a football ground. The carpets are plush and there's always a smell of polish in the air. Pictures of past heroes stare at you and under the stands there is room upon room stacked high with cups and trophies, as if you needed any reminding of their grand tradition.

We were met by United manager Ron Atkinson, who'd been with me at Albion up until the end of the season and the club chairman Martin Edwards. After the introductions, Tony and I sat down for talks with Mr Edwards while Denise went into Ron's office for a drink. Ron Atkinson never had anything to do with the actual talks about the terms, which might possibly surprise some people. I know that in West Bromwich a section of supporters thought, and probably still do, that Ron and I had been in league all summer over the transfer. They'd assumed that the first thing Ron did when he arrived at Old Trafford was to approach me behind everyone's back and get me to ask for a transfer, so United could move in. Nothing could have been further from the truth. I hadn't spoken to Ron Atkinson from the time he'd left the Midlands to the day of the transfer. Everything, as far as I was concerned, had been conducted in a proper manner. Ron was pretty unpopular in West Bromwich and I made him smile when I told him about the Albion fan who'd turned up at the Hawthorns just before I left that morning. He was calling Ron 'The thief of Old Trafford'. In his usual carefree manner Ron laughed it off and reckoned it had taken more than the word abracadabra to prise Albion open and persuade them to sell me. The talks with United chairman Martin Edwards were fairly brief and straightforward when you take into account how much money was involved. The only slight stumbling block, for a few minutes, was the length of contract. I wanted a five year agreement but United insisted, and rightly so, that I sign on for six years. As Mr Edwards pointed out they were spending a great deal of money and wanted to keep me for as long as possible. Ironically, although Tony Price and I had discussed my wages coming up in the car and settled on a figure to ask for, Mr Edwards jumped in before we had a chance to speak and offered more than we were going to ask. In ninety minutes everything was agreed and the next hurdle was the medical.

The medical used to be straightforward but recently

there had been several cases of transfers falling through because an X-ray or stringent check had revealed unknown injuries or weaknesses. With clubs spending so much money on one player it usually boils down to a question of insurance. No company in its right mind is going to cover a footballer with a dodgy knee for a million pounds or more, when one kick or nasty fall can put him out of the game. In my case I knew I was fully fit but there had been those three broken legs and the specialist paid great attention to them. Thankfully I sailed through with flying colours and apart from one or two minor details the transfer was settled.

United had hoped to complete the deal before 5 o'clock that afternoon, which meant I would be able to make my debut on the Saturday at Old Trafford against Wolves. We didn't make the deadline though, and it was decided instead, the transfer would be completed on the Saturday in front of fifty thousand fans on the pitch. The next day, Friday, I had my first taste of what being a United player was all about. That morning the club arranged a press conference at the ground. At Albion, I'd been used to facing a huddle of local reporters after training, or after a big game, so imagine my feelings when I walked into a room swamped with television lights and filled with fifty or more pressmen. The blinding lights made me feel like a man in front of a firing squad as the reporters took aim with their questions . . .

'What did it feel like to be valued at £1.8 million? Did it worry me? Would it put me under pressure? Was this the start of a new United?' They came thick and fast and after dealing with all those, there were endless interviews to do for television and radio.

One of the best bits of advice I was given early on in my playing career was never to be over-confident and make predictions that you weren't sure of fulfilling. So my answers were fairly straight and not too daring . . .

'It was a great feeling to be a Manchester United player. It's one of those things that every young football-loving lad dreams of. Who hasn't at one time in his fantasies played for Manchester United in front of a full house at Old Trafford and scored the winning goal?' I said the transfer fee didn't worry me, nor would it put pressure on me, which later I realized wasn't quite true. But I pledged my all for Manchester United and said it was up to me to prove that I was worthy of such a transfer fee.

Nobody of course is really worth £1.8 million because football transfer fees had really got out of hand. But United had dug deep into their pockets and even gone into the red to find the money and I was going to do my hardest to give some return on their investment. Denise in the meantime had gone back to West Bromwich to look after our daughter Claire and we both realized that the next few months would be lonely ones. We were obviously going to move to the Manchester area but, not knowing the north, it would take time to find somewhere suitable, which meant I would have to live away during the week and pop home on Sundays and days off. It was some time before we could get ourselves sorted out and go looking for a new home because there seemed so much to be done. On the Saturday it was the actual signing.

A crowd of just under forty-seven thousand packed into Old Trafford to watch United play Wolves. Whether you play for Manchester United or not, Old Trafford is one of every player's favourite grounds. With Albion I'd always looked forward to matches there because the atmosphere was so marvellous. The noise and excitement that boils up generates an immense feeling of pride and determination in any player, and when it came to walking out on the pitch before the match I realized just how much the fans expected of me. My name echoed around the vast stadium as I walked out with chairman Martin Edwards and manager Ron Atkinson. A table had been placed on the pitch and the first task was to sit down and actually sign the contract which completed the transfer and made me a part of United.

The cameras clicked and whirred as I signed and then I waved to the crowd. It was a strange feeling being dressed in a suit with shoes on because I'd much rather have been playing that afternoon, than sitting it out as a spectator. What an amazing feeling it was though as the Old Trafford crowd cheered and waved back. The red and white scarves fluttered in the wind and I must admit I wondered whether I was walking through a dream. As I waved to the crowd I thought I might feel myself falling out of bed and waking up with a bump back at home in Chester-le-Street with Mam calling me down for breakfast. This was no dream though and as I sat and watched United play against Wolves, I realized that I'd have to give everything I had and even a first team place could not be taken for granted the way they were blasting the opposition. United looked supreme as they went 2-0 up at half-time and finished off by thrashing Wolves 5-0. Although I was delighted to see United win so convincingly, I must admit that as I made my way downstairs after the game, I was a little worried about how Ron Atkinson would be able to change a side that had just won 5-0 in order to fit me in. I think one or two others, most of them in a half hearted fashion made similar comments afterwards. I may have been the country's most expensive footballer but I had no divine right to a first team place.

The first week at Old Trafford went fairly well. It helped knowing Ron Atkinson, his assistant Mick Brown and also another former Albion man Brian Whitehouse. He was on the training staff and of course it had been he who had given me my league debut with Albion. I also knew one or two of the players from the England squads and I managed quite easily to settle down. However, life at Old Trafford was in many respects totally different from Albion. At West Bromwich we used to report to the ground, get changed in the dressing rooms, train and then after a shower or bath make our way home.

At United we trained at the Cliff, the club's own training ground which is about ten minutes drive from Old Trafford. The Cliff has marvellous facilities. Apart from the training pitch there's an indoor gym for five-a-side and a fully equipped treatment room and a kitchen. United appeared to have more of a family atmosphere than Albion. After training, instead of disappearing, all the players went to the canteen for a meal and a pot of tea. This seemed to generate a better team spirit among the players as coaches, apprentices and reserves all sat down together.

Ron Atkinson and Mick Brown were running United on much the same lines as they had done at Albion. Mick would concentrate on the day-to-day training with Ron picking up players on some of the finer points, apart from taking part in the end of training five-a-side match. His enthusiasm for football is incredible and it had already rubbed off on to the United players.

My debut for United came on the Wednesday against Spurs in a League Cup tie at White Hart Lane. It was a close match and we could have hoped for more than a 1-0 defeat. I've certainly played better but my main aim was to adjust to the United style. My first league game for United could hardly have been a more demanding or crucial one, a local derby against Manchester City at

Maine Road. In West Bromwich I had played in local derbys for Albion against Wolves, Aston Villa and Birmingham City but the Manchester derbys are far more intense.

That first week everyone in the city seemed to be talking about the big game. From Monday onwards the local paper was looking ahead to Saturday. My league debut added even more fuel to the fire, as speculation mounted as to who United would leave out to make way for their new signing. Winger Steve Coppell was the unlucky man to be left out when the United team was named. I was down to play in my favourite number seven shirt in midfield. I must admit I felt sorry for Steve Coppell that weekend. After all there can't be too many players who've been dropped after their team has won 5-0. Manchester City's Maine Road ground was, not surprisingly, full to the rafters that Saturday as I proudly ran out in the famous red shirt of United. Local derbys are always important to players perhaps because they mean so much to the supporters. I'm sure in Manchester there are some football folk who'd be content for the rest of the year as long as their team won the derby. The game itself wasn't remarkable, like many local matches it was full of tension and the crowd could have been better rewarded than having to settle for a goalless draw. As for my baptism for United, well I was pleased. I felt I had made a good contribution to the team and had settled down well. I know I'd told people when I joined United that the transfer fee didn't worry me, but that's wrong, because it did. I didn't lose sleep, but I was well aware that because of the size of the fee, a lot was expected of me. In that first game against Manchester City every time I looked up a camera seemed to be pointed my way and I knew that my first game was going to come under close scrutiny.

I was confident within myself that I could settle with United and play my normal game but it perhaps took longer than I thought. The next week we drew at home to Birmingham City and I could feel myself getting more anxious. Because I was so keen to show United and their fans what I was capable of, I found myself running and running. I felt that I could help to justify the fee by running myself into the ground and giving everything I had. But by doing this my normal game suffered a little and it was a few weeks before I began to feel at ease.

Although the manager never puts any pressure on, you can feel it around you when arriving at the ground before a game, or even more afterwards if you haven't won. I had to win respect and prove myself to the people of Manchester and to the football world. Then a run of four wins, which included a thrilling 2-1 victory over Liverpool in front of their beloved Kop at Anfield and finishing in a 5-1 hammering of Sunderland at Roker Park, established United as first division leaders. What's more I'd scored against Sunderland so I felt at last that United and I were going to like each other.

Over the first few weeks it began to dawn on me just how much United meant in Manchester and the tradition and standing of the club. Wherever I went I was jumped upon by enthusiastic supporters wanting a quick chat or an autograph. One man who found himself without a piece of paper even whipped out his cheque book and asked me to sign it for him. People also pointed at me in the street and shouted encouragement in shops. I was waiting in the car at some traffic lights one day when a car pulled up alongside and blasted its horn. The passenger wound his window down, gave me the thumbs up and wished me well. Everyone it seemed wanted to be my friend and although it was nice to be made welcome I was happy to get back to the hotel which was my home for the first few months. Later I moved into a flat before settling down with Denise and Claire again in Cheshire. The first few weeks I missed my home most of all. I was happy with United but going back to a hotel room isn't fun and, when I could, I drove back to West Bromwich.

Apart from the United fans the club itself left me in awe and still does. Wherever you go at Old Trafford there are reminders of the great past. The Busby Babes of the fifties, the championship and European Cup winning days in the sixties. Names such as Duncan Edwards, Bobby Charlton, Denis Law and George Best seem to hang in the air. There are pictures of them adorning the walls and it is hard to hold a conversation about United without the name of Charlton or Busby cropping up. Some United players have felt intimidated or haunted by the club's golden image. Supporters are quick to compare players and teams with those of yesteryear and there's no doubt about it United and its supporters expect nothing but the best. When I first joined them I used to enjoy admiring some of the trophies on display at the ground and even now often walk round just for a look. The cups and medals and pictures of men like Charlton gave me inspiration early on, and still do. The likes of Edwards and Best will never be forgotten as long as football is played and my challenge was to get the present United team up on the wall alongside them. What it would be, I thought, to be in the company of such footballing greats.

The first time I met Bobby Charlton I realized that Manchester United is more than just a football club. His life has been United, and even now, he must be the club's number one fan. That's how it affects you. From the day I signed I felt an immense wave of pride in me every time I arrived at the ground, or ran out to play. It is such an overwhelming feeling to be playing for the greatest club side in the world. It was that pride and determination not to let the good name of United down that drove me on in the early days. I can remember reading in an old football book as a kid that 'The sheer presence of Manchester United is worth a goal start in any game because the name itself sends shivers down the opposition.' Well that may be an over-exaggeration but believe you me there's nothing like playing for the mighty Reds.

Apart from the pressure of the big money transfer, the other problem that worried me early on was the way I was branded in some quarters as a greedy money grabber. Back in West Bromwich a lot of supporters had the feeling I had let them down and moved to Manchester purely for a sack of gold. One or two local papers accused me of being disloyal and selfish. My answer was, and still is, very simple. If a chap working in an office or a factory is offered a better job, one that brings him more responsibility, a bigger challenge and better prospects and with it also more money surely most would accept the opportunity. Some admittedly would be content with their lot, but surely the majority would welcome the chance to improve and further their careers. Well that's exactly how I felt. Manchester United represented a better job for me. It brought me more responsibility, a much bigger challenge and on top of all that security for my family.

The chance to play for the biggest team in the country could not be turned down, and as far as Albion were concerned I had given them good service and what's more they weren't exactly giving me away. The money they got would help pay for the new stand or buy players for the team. One of the best stories to come out about this was of the reporter, who when I left Albion for United accused me of letting the side down. According to him I should have stayed. I read his article at the time and that was that. About a year later I discovered he'd left his local paper to work for one of the nationals. A few weeks later we happened to meet and jokingly I asked him why he had moved and wasn't he being disloyal to the local paper that had looked after him so well? His answer came with a shrug of the shoulders, 'Ah well Bryan, you know how it is!' We laughed together because I think he appreciated then why I left Albion. It was not just for the money. I had ambitions, and to me the chance to play for Manchester United was the way I was going to fulfil them.

# 9
# *More to Life than Football*

With the title of Britain's most expensive footballer came another I didn't expect – the most sought after.

I knew that playing for Manchester United would be different in that far more people follow the ups and downs of the club more closely. United, after all, are one of the standard-bearers for British football and everybody expects them to do well. One of the attractions of going to Old Trafford in the first place was to play for a bigger club, who had their sights firmly set on winning League Championships and other trophies. I realized the transfer would stir up a lot of interest but I thought that after a few weeks it would die down and the novelty of Britain's record transfer would wear off. So I was staggered when every other letter through the door and every phone call brought offers from enterprising businessmen who knew the profit there was to make out of a famous face or a well-known name. One of the hardest things I found as a young footballer was the way people in the street would recognize me and point, or in a shop I was embarrassed at first when I'd be browsing through some records or clothes and someone would come up and thrust a pen and paper under my nose and ask for an autograph. In time I got used to it, and then, later I learnt to cope with the press and the occasional interview for radio and television. When I first started playing in the Albion side the thought of being interviewed for radio or television used to terrify me. The first time somebody thrust a microphone at me I can remember my mouth going dry and all of a sudden the words started sticking in my throat. There were long pregnant pauses when my brain went blank, and only afterwards did I think of a hundred and one things I could have said. Television, as well, used to make me nervous with bright lights glaring into my face as the camera purred round. Some players love the publicity and the chance to talk, but with me, it was usually a pressgang job.

Over the years I have become more accustomed to it but that first press conference at Old Trafford still sent shivers up my back. It was not just the local papers and radio but BBC London was there, and so too was News at Ten. When I joined Ron Atkinson warned me that every move I made would be news because I was, in terms of transfers, the country's top footballer. When I joined Manchester United I hadn't really given much thought to anything but football. Admittedly I had an accountant who looked after the contract for me but I'd never really indulged in the commercial side of soccer that had grown so rapidly over the years.

At Albion I had opened shops and summer fairs and things like that, but I was never keen on pushing myself too much off the football field. I became more aware of football's other face with the England squad. Several players had contracts to wear a certain brand of boots or training gear, while the more successful were into advertising aftershave and other products. Quite a few wrote columns in papers and magazines or appeared regularly on television panels. This was a totally new world to me. As a young player I'd never given much thought to all this, concentrating instead on my game. But with the record transfer came increased pressure for me to spread my wings. Most of the Robson family are naturally cautious people and I've always been one to sleep on an idea or a decision instead of making a snap judgement and jumping in feet first.

When the offers to advertise this or sponsor that came rolling in I took meticulous notice of what and who were involved. In the first few months at Old Trafford, I was inundated with requests to advertise different types of sportswear and there were other offers from outside the game, such as modelling clothes. Most of them I turned down because, for one reason or another, they were not right. I've always been a great believer in putting your money where your mouth is, so I was reluctant, for the sake of a few hundred pounds, to endorse something I didn't really believe in. It would have been all too easy for me to grab the offers, but I was wary of people phoning me up or arranging meetings and treating me as though they were close friends. Some of the schemes that came forward were dubious and I decided that the best thing to do would be to settle down and then look more closely at the commercial side. I know that some of the football agents, whose job it is to promote players' careers off the field, thought I was missing out on a golden opportunity to cash in. Kevin Keegan, for so long this country's number one, was nearing the end of a glittering career and I think several businessmen were looking out for someone to take his place.

To me the important thing was to keep my feet firmly on the ground and not get carried away with all the glamour and trappings of playing for Manchester United and England. An awful lot of people, especially young kids, look up to footballers and other sports stars and I think it is important that they're set a good example. And that includes not tricking them that a certain football or sports shoe is far better than any other when you don't really know. The first major commercial deal I entered into after the move to Manchester was when I linked up with an American firm which manufactured running shoes. Several companies had approached me and asked if I would wear their boots and advertise them. In each case though, it was a question of just choosing one of their range and putting my name to it. This seemed somewhat hypocritical because I had strong feelings about the sort of boot I liked to wear, after all they're about the only tools a footballer ever has. When I suggested that they make one or two changes, the firms usually lost interest and reckoned they hadn't enough money to spend on developing new styles.

The American firm however were keen to hear my ideas on football boots. And so I drew up some suggestions for them. The main point was to produce a really comfortable boot, one that was simple, but also hard-wearing. I was flattered when they came back a few months later and said they were prepared to experiment with a prototype as long as I would agree to test it for them. I'd learned from several of the England players to be careful when entering into outside business deals. Several footballers have had their fingers burnt and lost their savings by wading into agreements and matters they don't understand and can't cope with. So, before I entered into my first commercial deal I got my accountant Tony Price to run a thorough check on the American firm. For all I knew they could have been some fly by night outfit, in the market for a quick killing. When the news came that the company was perfectly respectable and well established, I embarked on to the other side of football. At first I was a little worried because before now, I'd never had to concern myself with much else than playing football. Whereas most people have to worry about sales, or the production line at work, my only concern was the way I and United were playing.

So crossing the line into business was a big step. With a great deal of help and advice from the American company a new design for a boot was finally agreed upon and then the plans were taken back to America. A few months later the boots arrived and the idea was for me to wear them for at least a season to test them. The firm didn't want to gamble by marketing a product which was not up to scratch and at the same time I was reluctant to promote something I wasn't happy with or wouldn't wear.

For eighteen months I used the boots and after one or two adjustments here and there, they finally went into production. I was happy to be associated with them because they were something I believed in. The same sort of thing happened with footballs. Again I was approached and asked to put my name to a certain brand, but before I did, I got hold of a sample batch and gave them a good testing at the training ground and in the back garden. That's where I think footballers have made a mistake in the past. They think that playing for a big club or even being a professional footballer is like having a licence to print money. Some players have spent more time on their business interests outside the game than they have on training or preparing for a big match and I was determined that in my case football would always come first.

The move to Old Trafford also brought more demands on my private life and family. All football clubs attract hangers on. Supporters who like to mix with players and think they're friends with them and enjoy nothing better than trying to entice them into having a good time. One of United's favourite sons George Best was perhaps the best known victim of how football can turn sour if your head is turned by the other side of the game. I still find it hard to believe how George Best had the problems he did. When I met him he appeared to be a quiet, very down to earth sort of chap, who loved his football. How, I wondered, could such a man be responsible for some of the headlines and stories that shook Old Trafford and Manchester in the early seventies. I suppose his biggest problem was that he didn't have a wife or close family nearby to turn to, and when the party invitations came flooding in he got sucked up in the whirlwind of admirers. It would not be hard either because, in Manchester especially, a United or a City player commanded a lot of attention. When I first arrived at Old Trafford the invitations to go to parties and other functions poured in and it was amazing the number of people you'd meet who would greet you like a long lost friend. Although I enjoy a night out I've never been one for wild parties. A quiet drink and a nice meal out is my idea of a good night and although I enjoy mixing with football folk, most of my closest friends are nothing to do with the game. Most of them are from the West Bromwich area. People that Denise and I got to know when we used to live there, or from earlier days.

I think a good marriage and loyal friends are two of the most important things to a footballer. So much of your life is lived under the eyes of the public that it's pleasant to be able to get away and switch off. I know that when I first moved to Old Trafford I found it such a relief to drive home and be able to relax with Denise and Claire. And what a change it makes to a footballer to be able to go out and spend an evening without talking about the game.

There seems to be a popular belief that footballers are a race apart from other sportsmen and do nothing else but live and breathe it. Well I'm sure we all enjoy it, but I, for one, welcome the opportunity every now and then even if it's only for a couple of hours, to get away from soccer. Don't get me wrong. I don't mind people coming up and asking about United or England or supporters chatting about one thing or another, that's all part and parcel of being a professional footballer. What I do appreciate is an odd evening out when I don't have to go into discussions about United's chances in the league or how England is going to fare in the next big match. Fortunately Denise has never been a really keen soccer fan. She supported West Bromwich only because it was her home town team and of course took an interest in my career. The same goes with United. She supports them but is not one to travel miles to watch every single game. More often than not she's content to follow a match on radio or television and wait for my report when I get home. The same of our friends really. They all have a passing interest in football but appreciate there are other things in life. It makes me think of the great Bill Shankly of Liverpool and one of his favourite sayings. When asked if football was a matter of life and death to him he said it wasn't – it was far more important than that! But I go against that because when I became the country's most expensive footballer I realized the importance of having a settled family life and a strong circle of close friends. For a time after the transfer it was like living in a pressure cooker. Everybody wanted you, whether it was to build up a friendship, or embark on some business venture. Football has always been important to me and I suppose it always will be but there's so much more in life to enjoy as well.

# 10

# *England . . . The Gloom and the Glory*

Saturday, 30 July 1966 is a date emblazoned into the mind of every English football fan. It was the day England beat West Germany at Wembley to win the World Cup. As with all great moments in history I'm sure everyone can look back and remember what they were doing on that day. It was the middle of summer and the weather was more for cricket and tennis than football. If the Martians had landed that day in Chester-le-Street, or anywhere else come to that, they could have been forgiven for thinking they had discovered a ghost town. The shops were deserted and the streets empty as the nation sat in front of their television sets and watched the Wembley epic. In our house that day, dinner was extra early and the washing up had never been done in such speed as we rushed to take our places in front of the telly. It was in black and white and it was confusing to see England in the dark shirts while West Germany sported white. There was no mistaking the commanding figure of Bobby Moore though, or the toothless smile of Nobby Stiles as they lined up for the legendary battle.

We all sat enthralled as England pulled through to win 4-2 in extra time and you could hear the cheers from one end of the street to the other when the final whistle went. All the neighbours came out of their houses to celebrate, as passing cars hooted their horns in delight. That evening all the local lads made for the green for their own World Cup Final, but the only problem was that none of us wanted to be the Germans! Afterwards, I ran home

Bryan aged one

Chester-le-Street Junior Schools' Team 1967-8 – Bryan is holding the ball

Bryan aged 16 with his brother Justin

World Cup Qualifying Match June 1981. Bryan Robson is challenged by Hungarian defender Lazslo Balint; England won 3-1

Bryan is challenged by Manchester City's Martin O'Neill in his league debut for United, 10 October 1981

England *v* Northern Ireland 23 February 1982 and Bryan Robson celebrates after scoring the first goal after only 44 seconds. This was the quickest goal since 1951

1982 World Cup Finals. *Above right to left* Manager Ron Greenwood, Bryan Robson, Phil Neal and Coach Geoff Hurst take a rest during training. *Below* Terry Butcher congratulates Bryan who scored the first goal within the first minute of the match against France. England won the match 3-1

Bryan Robson outjumps Derby County captain Archie Gemmill; F.A. Cup Fifth Round, Derby County 0 Manchester 1, 19 February 1983

F.A. Cup Final 1983, Manchester United *v* Brighton. *Above* H.R.H. The Duke of Kent is presented to the United team by their captain, Bryan Robson. The match was a 2-2 draw. *Below* the replay was won by Manchester United 4-0 and Bryan Robson was presented with the Cup by H.R.H. Princess Michael of Kent

Gary Robson, Bryan's younger brother, who has followed in his brother's footsteps by playing for West Bromwich Albion

Bryan Robson, captain of England

On 20 August 1983 Bryan scored both of United's goals in the F.A. Charity Shield when they beat Liverpool 2-0

pretending I was one of the England men on a lap of honour around Wembley Stadium. I could hear the Wembley roar as I neared the front gate and that night I went to bed dreaming of our new national heroes. What it would be, I thought, to play for England in a World Cup Final.

The summer of 1966 came to me again when, as a member of the England squad, I sat on the plane bound for Spain and the 1982 World Cup. It was the end of my first season at Old Trafford and life since the transfer had been hectic. United had finished in third place in the first division behind champions Liverpool and Ipswich Town. I missed just one game and despite being nine points adrift from the title everyone at Old Trafford was pleased. We finished the season with a run of five wins in six games which included a 3-0 victory against West Bromwich Albion at the Hawthorns. Most of the transfer rumpus had died down by then and it was rewarding to score one of the goals. Away from football, our new home in Cheshire was being decorated and Denise was expecting our second child. The baby was due in the middle of the World Cup, so it was a strange feeling saying goodbye to Denise knowing that the next time we saw each other our family would have grown.

As we lifted above the clouds, all the players were thinking of the mission ahead. England had scraped through to the finals and an awful lot of supporters had written us off even before we landed in Spain. To some extent I was relieved the team was going out as underdogs. It was up to us to prove them all wrong. In Spain our first base was Bilbao in the north, and our first two games in the qualifying group against France and Czechoslovakia. Although there had been one or two rumours and stories about how unsuitable the town would be, since it was more an industrial centre, we settled in well at the luxury hotel which was to be our home for the next few weeks. Ron Greenwood, the England manager, and his staff had done a brilliant job on preparing for a long stay.

There was everything we wanted in the hotel and a whole host of activities to keep us occupied. Although the prospect of a few weeks in a five star hotel underneath the Spanish sun seems idyllic, it can get boring when you're locked in with a small group of people. And we were locked in. Around the hotel was a massive security net. Armed guards patrolled the grounds around the clock and we were not allowed to leave the complex on our own. The Spanish government, worried by the threat of terrorism, was taking no chances. If we went away from the hotel we had to be accompanied by an armed guard but they didn't really want us to leave and it was too much trouble to try to get through the manned checkpoint at the gate. So, we had to be content with snooker, table tennis, space invader machines and a wide choice of videos to keep ourselves occupied when we weren't training. On a couple of days we were allowed out for a game of golf. What an experience that was. I'm never at my best when there are people watching as I drive off the first tee outside the clubhouse, so imaginc what it was like trying to concentrate with a huddle of uniformed guards, armed to the teeth with rifles, breathing down your neck. The course record wasn't broken that day, but after a time we got used to it and I give full marks to the Spanish government for taking such precautions.

In Bilbao the England squad was settled and it showed. We swept France aside 3-1 in the opening match with two of the goals coming my way. Next we beat Czechoslovakia 2-0 but in this match I limped off towards the end and was replaced by Glen Hoddle. Injury kept me out of the third qualifying game against Kuwait but it was another victory. We managed to beat them 1-0 and although there were one or two sticky moments, everybody felt England was on its way at last. Next stop was Madrid and the quarter-final stage. Before leaving Bilbao though, I was introduced to our new daughter Charlotte. It was early morning when my father-in-law rang through from West Bromwich to tell me Denise had had the baby and both were in the best of health. Later on I managed to chat with Denise over the phone and was feeling elated as the squad sat down for their evening meal. There were congratulations all round and then something out of the ordinary happened. Earlier in the day I'd done an interview for ITV and was surprised when they came back that night to ask if they could do another because there was a fault on the film. We sat on a settee facing a television and the lads said they were going to ask me to comment on some action. Much to my amazement and delight the video they were showing me wasn't of England playing but of my wife and baby daughter. The television boys had filmed Denise and little Charlotte in hospital earlier in the day and then beamed the pictures over to Spain. It was a marvellous moment as I sat thousands of miles away watching my new baby daughter.

Those happy memories though were left as we set off for Madrid and the next stage of the World Cup Competition. We had to face West Germany, one of the favourites and England's arch rivals, and the host country Spain. We couldn't have had a tougher draw, so, as we travelled south, the pressure began to mount.

Our stay in Madrid wasn't as happy as the stop in Bilbao and I think this could have affected us. The squad didn't seem to settle as well in our new hotel, it was busier and noisier and not as comfortable. In Bilbao our headquarters had been a home from home but in Madrid it was not as welcoming. One aspect of the World Cup which surprised me was the number of press and television men that used to surround the hotel. In England, or even on foreign trips you get to know the faces, but in Spain there were hordes of them. Reporters from as far away as Hong Kong and Brazil came up and asked for interviews and the interest in the finals was staggering.

Our success in the qualifying round had given us a difficult path through to the semi-finals. We had won both of our matches and had got stuck with West Germany and Spain, while the team that finished behind us, France, got the easier pairing of Northern Ireland and Austria. In our last match against the Czechs I'd gone off with a knock and after some smart work by the England physio Fred Street was passed fit for the match against the West Germans. It was played in Madrid's Bernabeu Stadium, one of the most breathtaking grounds in the world. We expected a hard match and got it. Desperately we looked for the goal to give us a hold on the Germans but it just wouldn't come. We held them well but I think all of the England lads felt we should have got more than a goalless draw. Three days later West Germany played Spain and beat them 2-1 so everything was riding on the last game between ourselves and the host nation.

If we were to reach the semi-finals we had to win by two clear goals. As the preparations got underway the spotlight was turned on Ron Greenwood who faced what was possibly the biggest dilemma as England manager. The captain, Kevin Keegan, and midfield man Trevor Brooking hadn't played yet in the finals because they were both carrying injuries. Now they were fit and Greenwood had to decide whether to keep an unchanged team or bring back two of his most trusted and experienced men. It was

Catch 22. If he played Keegan and Brooking and we lost then the fans would say he should never have played them but instead kept the same team. If he didn't play them and we lost then they'd blame him for not bringing the two into the side. I'm sure it must have weighed heavily on his mind and he decided to hedge his bets by keeping an unchanged team but included both Keegan and Brooking amongst the substitutes. Kevin, I know, was bitterly disappointed. He'd done so much for England over the years and he realized that Spain would be his last chance for World Cup glory.

The venue was again the Bernabeu Stadium and although England had a healthy following in Madrid, the ground that night was awash with Spanish flags. We knew we'd be taking on over seventy thousand fanatical Spaniards apart from their national team and with so much at stake, it was a tense game to play in. Both sides held back a little hoping to strike on the break. We had our chances and in the second half Ron Greenwood brought on both Keegan and Brooking in the hope they'd find something special with which to surprise Spain who were as desperate as us for victory. When the whistle went I looked up to the giant electronic scoreboard and there it was Spain 0 England 0 . . . both of us had failed.

What a distraught night that was in Madrid. All the players were broken and Ron Greenwood tried desperately to gee us up by telling everyone how well they'd done. We knew though and so did he, that this was the parting of the ways. It was an open secret that Greenwood was stepping down as England manager after the World Cup Finals, and he'd come to the end of the road.

On paper, England's world cup campaign wasn't a bad one; we'd played five matches, won three and drawn two, but the most galling thing was we'd scored six goals and conceded only one. England were on their way home having given only one goal away and not lost a match, somehow it didn't seem fair. It was after the Spanish game that the England team had one of its most terrifying experiences. After we changed we were bustled out on to the coach and you can imagine the sense of disappointment in the streets of Madrid that night, with Spain out of the World Cup. We'd been given a pretty hostile departure from the pitch, but as we drove back through the streets to our hotel, the local people booed and jeered. The police ordered us to lie down on the seats and at all costs keep away from the windows. As the coach crawled through the packed streets of football supporters, there were loud bangs and crashes against the side of the coach and we were mighty relieved to get back to our rooms in one piece.

Some players chose to stay on in Madrid for a few days' holiday, others drifted off to meet their families in other foreign climes for a holiday while the rest of us returned home. Going to Spain had been a tremendous experience and on the way home I vowed to myself that next time we would be there in the final.

The World Cup was the end of another era for English international football. Ron Greenwood departed and in his place came Bobby Robson, the natural successor. We all realized changes were on the way, but quite a few were in for a shock. One of the first major moves Bobby Robson made was to make Ray Wilkins, my United pal, the captain and give me the vice-captaincy. We were in the same role at Old Trafford and I welcomed the extra responsibility.

A casualty, though, was Kevin Keegan. I think it was a mistake on Bobby Robson's part to leave Keegan out so soon. The decision came as a surprise, especially to Kevin, who was rather hurt by the swiftness of it all. He'd served his country well and fully expected at least another couple of seasons at international level. Keegan is a true professional and sets a marvellous example to all. In training he would often try to help with advice or special tips and he was a man whom most of the England squad looked up to and admired. For these reasons Bobby Robson should have kept him on a little longer. Even if he did not plan to use him, the presence of Keegan in an England squad was invaluable. British tennis teams usually have a non-playing captain who is there to help, guide and coach the squad, and I believe Keegan should have been used in this way. As a senior professional he would have helped to encourage and advise the younger players. Keegan was a man we all learned from, and his sudden departure left quite a gap. On the other hand, Bobby Robson wanted to build his team and rightly pointed out that it was the future and the 1986 World Cup which had to be in our sights. It was encouraging to see the younger players brought into the squad as the manager set out on a policy to test the talent of English football.

One of the biggest shocks the England players had was in the change of lifestyle. In the past we'd always stayed at the sumptuous West Lodge Park Hotel in Hertfordshire. The hotel was a palace inside and was set in the most picturesque grounds you could imagine. We lived like kings there before international matches and we could have anything we wanted. If you were thirsty or a little hungry late at night you knew a phone call to the kitchen would bring a cup of tea and a sandwich. Our shoes were polished, and our clothes dry cleaned. In fact we were spoiled and pampered, and treated as family. So, when Bobby Robson announced that the luxury of West Lodge was being done away with and the squad would be staying at Bisham Abbey training centre, there were several frowns amongst the players. Bisham is a wonderful training centre, with spectacular facilities but the accommodation is somewhat spartan compared to a luxury hotel. Meals are taken in a canteen, there are no late night snacks or waiter service. Television has to be watched in a communal lounge and the bedrooms are more like army barracks. I think, in principle, Bobby Robson had the right idea because life could be a little too easy at West Lodge, but most of the players felt he was moving from one extreme to the other and after a couple of sessions at Bisham, I think he realized this as well. We still use the Abbey as a training centre but sleep and eat in a hotel down the road. The Robson revolution was underway, and within a very short time, I found myself called on to the bridge and given the captaincy of the ship. Ray Wilkins was out injured and, as at United, I was asked to step into his shoes and take over.

To be captain of Manchester United and England was as near perfection as possible. I'd always wanted to be a footballer and had ambitions to play for my country. But to end up as captain of both club and country was unbelievable. The role of captain is one I enjoy immensely. Ever since my schooldays I've been a player who likes to shout in football. A lot of people don't realize the importance shouting can make on a football field. A well-marshalled defence is one controlled by a goalkeeper, telling his defenders exactly where to go, while it's important the whole team is kept on its toes. As captain it's vital you understand the players around you. It's no good shouting your head off and complaining when things are not going right. There are some players who respond to a few sharp words, while others wilt and become disheartened if you're too harsh with them. Alternatively, encouragement and praise can lift some players who are struggling. The hardest part about being a captain is you feel guilty if you're not leading by example. As the skipper I feel I have to set an example and when I'm struggling to find form I find it difficult to start having a go at others for making mistakes. That's why it helps to have other experienced players around you. They know when things aren't going right for you and come to the rescue by taking the weight off your shoulders.

Of all the England players I've been with I think Terry McDermott, who was an integral part of the great Liverpool team, did more than anyone else to make me a better player. Terry is a good pal of mine. He's a great character and with England was the clown prince. Even Ron Greenwood would be in tucks of laughter when Terry started cracking jokes and telling his stories. But he was also a brilliant player. Ironically, at Liverpool, he was one of our biggest rivals, but he taught me to score a lot of goals.

There was a time when I used to rush towards goal and as soon as I saw an opening and the chance to shoot, blast the ball forward. After an England training session Terry tried to point out where I was going wrong. When the chance to shoot came I should just pause for a second and instead of simply cracking the ball towards the target, try to vary the finish. I was, he reckoned, too predictable. Well, whenever I could I watched Terry and as soon as I studied him the message sank home. I recorded lots of Liverpool matches on video and played them over and over again. McDermott was, perhaps for a midfield player, one of the finest finishers there's ever been. He would get through and then instead of doing the obvious might try and lob the ball over the keeper's head or carefully place it. It might sound a little obvious but it's amazing how many midfield players don't give enough thought to this part of their game. They use their craft to create openings for others but when a goal stares them in the face, they swing a boot and hope for the best. After watching those videos I tried to use the McDermott method and suddenly I found myself scoring more goals than ever. A split second to look up and think of something different worked wonders.

I'm sure that with Bobby Robson at the helm the England team will rise again and we'll be able to emulate those heroes of 1966. There's no reason why England shouldn't win the next World Cup. Our players are amongst the best in the world, and by the time we reach 1986 the manager should have a well-balanced team.

A question that's always asked is why the national team has failed in the past, when sides such as Liverpool, Forest and Villa have won the European Cup. In England most of our time and energy is put into league and cup football and international matches are slotted in here and there. Quite often injuries play havoc with the side and I for one have suffered from too much football. I'm sure Bobby Robson wonders if I have some sort of grudge against him, the way injuries always catch me when a major game comes along. It would be easy to patch myself up and play when not fully fit but then you are cheating, not only yourself, your England colleagues, but also the fans.

To win the World Cup Final needs time. I think some people tend to lose sight of the fact that when the Brazilians or Argentinians prepare for a big tournament they plan months in advance. The squad are taken off to the country and train and live together for anything up to two months. So when the match comes along they're fully prepared and are a well regimented unit. By comparison England spend two or three days together every two months or so and it's quite an achievement for the manager to be able to call on all of his players. There's always a running battle between the England manager and club managers about releasing players for internationals. The club manager has his league position and cup run to worry about and is reluctant to release his players in case they should get injured. The England manager meanwhile, is trying to pick his best side and build a team together, so that when the World Cup comes around he's ready. Players are left in the middle of a tug of war. Everyone loves playing for his country, but then you are under contract to your club. I approach the dilemma simply. If I'm fit I'll play anywhere if selected.

If England is to rise again as a powerful soccer nation and put itself on a par with Brazil we have to look very seriously at giving more time to the cause. It's no good going away for a few weeks before a World Cup Final because the preparations have to be long term. Why not devote a whole month of the year, say May or June or even August to international football? The players of England, Scotland, Wales and Ireland would be freed from their clubs for that time and there would be no other call on them. At least it would give the international managers a chance to really get to know their players and for the individuals to knit together.

As with other aspects of football, we have to start making changes. So often decisions are made, and policies carried out under the banner of saying 'it's the way it's always been done'. The England hierarchy must act now. They must push for changes and the football league should respond accordingly.

People in football should be more far-sighted. When England won the World Cup back in 1966 it brought a surge of interest back into the game. Another World Cup win would have the same effect. So before it's too late, let's start planning now and say to ourselves England is going to win the World Cup. We have the players, so let's give ourselves a fighting chance. Winning the World Cup, I suppose, is my ultimate ambition although I know my Mam fondly dreams of a day when there'll be more than one Robson in the team. (Bobby, the manager, is no relation, I hasten to add.)

The Charltons came from the same neck of the woods as us and I know Mam and Dad have always wondered whether their boys could all be playing for the England team one day. What a midfield it would be . . . Gary Robson, Justin Robson and Bryan Robson. Justin had an unlucky start to his career. He signed for Newcastle United and seemed to have settled down well. But after one or two setbacks he was discarded on a free transfer and has a long fight ahead of him. He's a fine player mind you but perhaps lacks the bite of our youngest brother Gary who followed me to West Bromwich Albion. Gary has always been one of the most determined and single-minded in the family, and is fast making his mark at the Hawthorns. I think the following story best sums him up. The first England cap I had I gave to my parents but after a few internationals I decided to offer one to my brothers and sister. When I came to give one to Gary, he politely but firmly turned the offer down. 'Thanks for thinking of me Bryan, but I want to win my own. I must have something to go for.' With determination like that, how can he fail? Good luck to him. Whenever I can, I pass on advice to Gary, but honestly, I think it's better to let him make his own way. I'm glad I'm not the younger brother, because he must get sick and tired of being compared to me. As soon as everybody realized he was my brother his name couldn't be mentioned without mine. Some Albion fans will tell you he's a better player than I was at his age and I hope from now on they judge him as Gary Robson and not Bryan's little brother. I think comparisons are made so much because our style and approach is very similar. With the Charltons it was different. Jack was tall and a powerful centre-half, while Bobby was smaller and either a midfield player or a front runner. I only hope that, like the Charltons, the Robson lads will get the chance to play together for England one day.

# 11
## *Captain's Choice*

Walk into any pub or club anywhere in the country and I bet that in a corner somewhere you'll find people talking football. It's a subject that draws folk together. At times they argue about their local teams or certain players or reminisce over great games they've seen.

Although I was only six at the time one of the first major matches I can remember was the one at Wembley between England and the Rest of the World in 1963. It was played to celebrate the centenary of the Football Association and was shown live on television in the afternoon. On arriving home from school I dashed in to watch and was caught by the magic of the game. The Rest of the World seemed such a grand title and to actually see players such as the Russian keeper Yashin, the dashing De Stefano, the brilliant Eusebio and the legendary Puskas in action was a dream.

One of the popular pastimes of players and fans alike is to pick their favourite teams, whether it be the best Manchester United team of all time or a World eleven, and often people come up to you in pubs or restaurants and want to know what you think of one player or another. Well to settle a few arguments, how about a British eleven? Before I start, I'm afraid I'm going to be England biased, because I feel happier judging players I've actually been alongside with in a game.

So, putting on my hat as the British manager let's start with a goalkeeper; three obvious candidates are Peter Shilton, Ray Clemence and Pat Jennings. All have very different styles. Shilton would get my vote because I think he is without doubt the best goalkeeper I have ever seen. His attitude is perfect and his professionalism unbeatable. Shilton is a perfectionist. Even when he walks into a dressing room after keeping a clean sheet he will sit and think over the match and dwell on the smallest mistake or miscalculation. In training he will work for hours on his angles and leaves nothing to chance. Physically he is a giant of a man and his sheer presence dominates the goal area. It's so important to a team to have such a man at the back and I'd have Shilton every time. Ray Clemence is also a brilliant keeper and perhaps has more natural ability and agility than Shilton but doesn't seem to possess the same dominance. Pat Jennings is a tribute to himself as he nears the forty mark. The Irishman has a style all of his own and he's got to be one of the best keepers of all time, but he's not as good as Shilton.

Now to the defence. As I'm picking a team of the most recent players I would go for Liverpool's Phil Neal at right-back. I'm sure thousands would argue against his selection because for some strange reason Phil's a player who has never won the acclaim he deserves. He always seems to be made the scapegoat if England fails and outside of the players, it's hard to find anyone with a good word for him. The fans don't seem to rate him and the press have been trying for years to find another right-back. But having played alongside Phil with England, he takes some beating. He's a far better player than many give him credit for and in choosing Phil Neal I make two very relevant points. First of all can you name another right-back with as much experience and skill and secondly what about his record? Bad players simply don't manage to hold on to their places in a team such as Liverpool which has swept the world, neither do they play for their country. There are one or two youngsters, Danny Thomas of Spurs and United's talented Mick Duxbury who spring to mind, but in the past there have been others who have tried to take Phil Neal's place and failed.

At left-back I'd have Kenny Sansom. After one or two hesitant games at international level he seems to have settled down well and improves with every game. As well as being a reliable defender he likes to attack and does so with great speed and success. My old Albion team mate Derek Statham has been unlucky not to get more international chances, but injuries seem to have burdened him over the last couple of seasons, otherwise he would be my choice. To make up the back four I'd have Dave Watson at centre-half and alongside him Mark Lawrenson of Liverpool. Watson is my idea of a number five. He looks the part as a tall, wide shouldered man and his power is undeniable. As with the goalkeeper, it's vital to have an experienced and reliable man at the heart of defence. Watson is without doubt the best centre-half English football has seen in years. Apart from being strong in the air he is quick on the ground and there is nobody to touch him. Another man who came into the reckoning was Gordon McQueen of Manchester United and Scotland. McQueen is a fine player and has served his country well, but Watson has the edge. The number six shirt is a more difficult one to fill. Looking back over the last few years there have been several who would claim a place. From Liverpool and Scotland there's Allan Hansen. He's done a grand job for his team, but on one or two occasions I've seen him make mistakes or bad judgements. He's still a good player but I think his team mate Mark Lawrenson is a better one. He seems to play with more confidence and his agility and speed quite often prove too much for opponents. The Ipswich pairing of Terry Butcher and

Russell Osman provides quite a team but I still think they need some extra experience. One player whom I've always admired is Colin Todd. If it had not been for the impeccable Bobby Moore or that great competitor Norman Hunter, Colin would surely have been a regular with the England team. For a defender his skill was amazing and he could read a situation perfectly. The only thing about him was he seemed to lack ambition or that killer instinct. So, with Shilton in goal, we would have Neal, Watson, Lawrenson and Sansom in front.

Now for midfield. First I would have Glen Hoddle of Spurs. I think he is a fabulous player and one who still hasn't fully achieved his real potential. On his day Glen must be one of the finest players in the world. He has that rare ability of being able to win or influence a match on his own. At international level he perhaps hasn't played as well as he can, but for Spurs he's provided some memorable moments. When I first started on the international trail the last place in midfield was usually down to me or Glen. He got the vote at first because as one paper put it: 'The England manager has gone for the unquestionable skills of Hoddle rather than the breathtaking endeavour and enthusiasm of Robson.' Well every man to his own, but Hoddle is an artist, of that there is no doubt. I think in his case an England manager has to have patience and let Hoddle play his natural game. He's not a man to whom you can give specific instructions, he's more of a player who has to be left alone to do his own thing. Alongside Glen I would have my United pal Ray Wilkins. He was another player who arrived on the international scene at about the same time. Having played with Ray at all levels of football from youth international to league and cup football I feel qualified to say there are not many finer men around. When I arrived at Old Trafford he was the captain and was later made the England captain as well. Injury forced him out of the United team, and I was lucky enough to take over both as skipper of England and United.

I think this intrigued many people because they assumed we were deadly rivals and that Ray would be upset by being deposed at Old Trafford by me. He had to fight to win his place back in the United team but when he did there was no stopping him. Ray Wilkins has been one of my greatest friends at Old Trafford. We play well alongside each other, and on the field he's perhaps my biggest influence. As a captain it's hard to shout at others when you are having a bad game yourself. The beauty of having Ray with you is that he's quick to realize this, and will take some of the responsibility off my shoulders to allow me to concentrate on my own game.

The way Ray came back into the United side and the England team and won people round with some staggering displays is a great credit to him as a footballer. Many players in Ray's position would have demanded a transfer and looked for a first-team place elsewhere. But, like everybody at Old Trafford, he took pride and joy from playing with United and refused to accept the easy way out. Over the past two years Ray has been one of the key figures in the United revival and at international level as well he's proved his brilliance. Apart from being a fine competitor, Ray's main strength is that he keeps his head and game going when the team is struggling. He never panics and when heads start to droop, Ray is still going at full steam, not only pushing his own game, but encouraging those around him. He's not a fussy or fancy player but watch him closely and try to spot how many mistakes he makes. You'll have a hard time!

The other midfield berth would go to the grand old man

of West Ham, Trevor Brooking. There can't have been many more stylish players. He amazes me because he always makes everything look so easy. Trevor's so clever at reading a game or a situation, and so quick to react that he expends half the energy of anyone else. When you look around, the rest of the team seem to be puffing and panting while Trevor's standing there looking as fresh as a daisy. Apart from his stylish performances on the field, Trevor is another man who is a shining example to all away from the game. He's a very intelligent and easy going sort of chap who has great influence on any team he is with. I've always tended to look on Trevor as one of the wise old men of the England squad, the sort of chap you would turn to if ever in trouble. He meets his challenges square on and invariably has a smile on his face and a friendly word for everyone. He's not the sort of chap to go shouting the odds, opting instead to do things in his own quiet, gentlemanly manner. Football and the first division could do with a few more like him.

Now to the attack, and although there's a long list of goalscorers to choose from, the front three, I think, pick themselves. Kenny Dalglish of Liverpool and Scotland, former England skipper Kevin Keegan, and the first man to be sold for a million pounds, Trevor Francis.

Dalglish I pick because, without doubt, he has been one of the key men in the Liverpool success story. His speed and finishing are nothing short of incredible. He can shield a ball better than anyone and is a real match-winner. Although he's a hard worker, Dalglish can take only seconds to turn a match upside down. For eighty-nine minutes you can watch him being tackled and marked closely but give him one split second opening and he's there. And, knowing that his chances have to be taken, the little Scot rarely makes a mistake. He's one of the hardest opponents to play against because you know he'll never give up, and will always try something different to find a way through to goal. Keegan too, is an automatic choice because, like Dalglish, he has that quality of being able to turn a game single handed. His experience of both top flight English and European football would be a must in any British side and he is one of the few players of world class that we have produced in recent years. Keegan is a man for the big occasion. He soaks up the atmosphere of Wembley so well and thrives on pressure. Keegan has style, and we need more like him to keep football going. In the sixties people such as Bobby Charlton, George Best, Jimmy Greaves and Denis Law were great crowd pullers. Fans would be prepared to go to a game just to watch them, no matter who the opposition was. Well, Keegan is one of the few players who has inherited that quality. If Keegan plays, he can put thousands on the gate, as he has done at Southampton and Newcastle. He has star quality, but what's more can play and is a man who can take goals from either three yards out or thirty.

The third man is Trevor Francis. In many respects he is a similar sort of player to both Keegan and Dalglish. One who can be tied down by close marking for much of the game, but give him the smallest of chances and he takes it. I think Trevor's main problem is that he's light years ahead of his time. Dalglish and Keegan are great movers but Francis has an amazing ability to turn on the ball. It seems at times as though he is made of rubber when he twists in and out of defenders and around lunging tackles. In many respects Trevor is too fast, and has paid the penalty with a long list of injuries. He takes an enormous amount of kicks and punishment and yet most of it is down to his own brilliance. He is just too quick and by the time defenders have realized what he's doing their tackle aimed at the ball only succeeds in bringing Trevor crashing to the floor.

Without so many injuries Trevor Francis would have rivalled Jimmy Greaves or Bobby Charlton as one of England's greatest goalscorers. It's easy to look around and come up with a long list of possibles to play in the attack, but Francis has real class. It's a shame his talents were exported to Italy. Like Keegan he was attracted to the challenge of European football and perhaps became a little disillusioned with the first division. English football can't afford to lose players like Francis to the continent because, if our game is to survive and pull the crowds in, we need his sort of player over here.

Before shutting the door on my British team, it would only be fair to assess some of the other contenders. First Charlie Nicholas, the golden boy from Scotland who's brought London to life since he moved to Arsenal last summer. Nicholas is a quality player and takes his chances well. With Celtic he was undoubtedly a roaring success, but I haven't chosen him, because it's hard to judge him on just one season of English football. Like Dalglish he has tremendous close control and is the sort of player I would hate to mark, he is never still, always trying a different approach to find a way to goal. John Wark of Ipswich and Scotland nearly got into my team, because I admire his relentless pushing and driving. He is a very capable player but also a consistent goalscorer. Although he hasn't the class of say Wilkins or Hoddle, he is a very adaptable player.

In the attack I've not chosen a winger or a big old fashioned centre-forward. They are useful on occasions, but I prefer the more skilful type. I've never really been all that keen on wingers. As I said, at times they can be useful but also frustrating. With wingers a side can be predictable. An attack is slowly constructed and then the ball is pumped out to the wing. He makes for the line and swings across a high looping centre for the tall striker. I know it was popular in years gone by but we have to change and go along with the rest of the football world. Steve Coppell at United I rated highly, but he was more adaptable and didn't always hug the line. At Albion, playing with Peter Barnes on the wing could be frustrating. His talents were unquestionable, but Peter used to take a little too long sometimes in beating his man and getting the ball across. By the time the centre arrived the element of surprise had gone and any opening had been closed. The two most effective wingers I ever saw were Peter Thompson and Ian Callaghan of Liverpool. They suited Liverpool's play in those days, and were so quick and accurate with their crosses or shots that they became the scourge of every defence.

There are many centre-forwards to choose for a team. Paul Mariner is one player whom I think is given a hard time. People tend to write him off too quickly as a bit of a blunderer who manages to score a few goals. Well, not every top player has delicate ball skills and with somebody like Paul Mariner you only have to look at his goalscoring record to make a proper assessment. His name is rarely off the scoresheet at Ipswich and he's got his share for England as well. Peter Withe is another player for whom I've got a lot of time. Like Mariner he is always regarded as being a big physical player who bumps and barges his way around the football field. But with Francis at Forest and then Gary Shaw at Aston Villa, he struck up remarkable partnerships. Withe is an unselfish player who will run and work until he drops trying to succeed. His main strength is the way he can lay balls off, or set opportunities up for his colleagues. Whether it be a head, chest or knee

Peter Withe creates some great openings and is another player far better than many give him credit for. Cyrille Regis, a striker I know well from my days at West Bromwich Albion, is another who possibly does not get the acclaim he deserves. Regis is wrongly regarded by many as a bustling and physical player but he's got far more skill and intelligence than most.

Of the younger players coming up, Villa's Gordon Cowans looks a gem. I was worried at first that he was too slight to battle in midfield but Cowans is a determined player who fights until he wins. He's got great ball skills as well, and in two or three years will be a force to be reckoned with. Steve Hodge at Nottingham Forest is another player who really impressed me recently. He has pace, good control and a lively football brain, which I'm sure will help England out in the near future.

In choosing a British team I've tried to select a side that could play skilful and entertaining football. There seems to be a worrying shift towards the old kick and rush style and if too many teams adopt it our football will suffer badly. When you look at the names there are to choose from, it's difficult to understand why England or Scotland haven't got nearer to winning the World Cup. Surely it won't be long before a home side does it again. I'm sure Robson's XI, with everybody fit, would give sides such as Brazil, Italy and West Germany a run for their money.

# 12
## *The Managers*

'Don't put your daughter on the stage Mrs Worthington' is a wonderful song which captures all the dangers and worries for parents of a young hopeful embarking on a theatrical career. It's a wonder by now, that no one has come up with an equivalent rhyme for football.

The job of a football manager must be one of the most daunting and demanding there is in sport. He has to be a jack of all trades, and master of them as well. Apart from his knowledge of football he has to be able to manage people, from the players down to the groundsmen. He also needs an astute mind to deal with transfer and contract negotiations involving millions of pounds. He has to be an ambassador for the club as well as a public relations expert to deal with the press.

When you look at how much work gets dished on to a manager's plate you realize why the rewards for success are great. On the football side of the job he has to run three or four teams, overseeing all the training and coaching, and at the same time has to be on the lookout for any up and coming youngsters, or better players to keep the side ticking over. When your team is winning it must be a tremendously satisfying job, but when you're losing it can be a lonely and desperate existence.

What qualities are needed to be a manager? Well, he has, of course, got to know his football and preferably have played as a professional. Managers who were players always seem to exert more authority and confidence in their team. There are exceptions of course, take Laurie

McMenemy at Southampton. He was really a non-league player, but nobody would doubt his talent or success as a manager. Others have tried to bridge the gap but have usually failed because in many ways, football is like a family. Outsiders have to prove themselves before they are admitted and accepted. But it doesn't always follow that good players make it as managers. Looking down the first division most of the top managers, Ron Atkinson, Keith Burkinshaw of Spurs and Aston Villa's Tony Barton for example, were never great names on the field, but have progressed well into management using their knowledge and love of the game. On the other hand, men such as Bobby Charlton, Geoff Hurst and Martin Peters, all members of England's World Cup winning team were never successful managers.

I think the most important ingredient for a manager to have is being able to communicate and work with those around him. It's amazing how many seem incapable of dealing with their players. Apart from football, they have to cope with all sorts of problems, as players usually take all their worries to him. It might be about wages, buying a house, or occasionally a manager has to try his hand at marriage counselling. What a life! It still surprises me how many keep coming back for more punishment, after they've been sacked or forced to resign from a team. I suppose the feeling is, that sooner or later their luck will change and it will be their turn to lead a side out at Wembley. The manager I know best of all is, of course, Ron Atkinson. I followed him from Albion to Old Trafford and over the years we've struck up a good relationship. He's a strong minded man who knows what he wants and invariably gets his way. Ron Atkinson has probably got where he is because he's a gambler, a man not afraid of making decisions and one who never sits on the fence.

When he makes his mind up or decides on a certain policy he'll put everything he has into making sure he's done the right thing.

One of Ron's most appealing strengths is that he's a great man to have on your side. Some managers I know can be unpredictable and blow with the wind, leaving you wondering. Atkinson though is a manager who backs his players and will stand up and defend them. It's rare for him to criticize players in public. On occasions he's had a go at the team, or an individual in the privacy of the dressing room, only to walk outside and defend them. Players appreciate him for that. There can be nothing more distasteful than a manager who says nothing to his players and then attacks them in public. What does a player do? If he retaliates and has his say, he can be fined for speaking out of turn. Thankfully Ron is a fair manager who is always prepared to listen. If ever there's an argument, or discussion about some point of play, you are allowed to put your own case forward and you know it will be considered. Ron loves his football, as I suppose most managers do, and will sit for hours on a coach or plane journey swopping stories about famous teams or players. He loves being with his players. I think he enjoys the camaraderie of the dressing room and I wonder at times whether he is in danger of getting too close to us. It's important for a manager to mix with his men, but he must also be detached.

A manager has to keep the respect of his players and there are times when he has to lay down the law, so, if he allows himself to get too close it becomes more difficult for him to enforce decisions he makes. Players must always regard a manager as their boss, and there must be a dividing line between them.

Ron Atkinson has made quite a name for himself at Old

Trafford and the popular belief outside the game is that he's a bit of a 'Champagne Charlie'. There are whole articles written about the amount of jewellery he wears and the way he dresses. His image though has been blown out of proportion, the way that cartoonists accentuate the characteristics of politicians and other leading public figures. If you're a cabinet minister with a larger than average nose or a splendid set of teeth, then more often than not you are depicted as some strange animal with a six foot nose and teeth like tombstones. In Ron's case it was noticed that he liked wearing a gold bracelet on his wrist and a couple of rings. Suddenly he was depicted as a chap with a jeweller's shop on each hand and the crown jewels on his wrist and around his neck. If you take a close look at Ron, he doesn't wear that much and the same goes for his champagne image. Again, you'd think by the way some people talk that he gets through a crate of champagne a day. Ron likes to live in style and enjoy life. When he first arrived at Albion, his colourful ways really livened up the place. He was adventurous and his bubbling manner was a change. Albion were a little old fashioned, and I think some of the directors used to frown at the way Ron celebrated with a bottle of champagne or two after big matches. It was as though some young whipper snapper had disturbed the peace and quiet by pulling down the curtains, switching the lights on and turning the music up. But his ways really lifted Albion. The players began to think that they could win major trophies, and were as good as their counterparts at Liverpool and Spurs. In time, I think Ron realized his ambitions were not matched by the Albion directors and when the chance came to take over United he jumped at it. United and Atkinson are a wonderful pairing. The club wants success and the stylish Atkinson is just the man to project and promote the image, I don't think he's changed from his first job as manager of non-league Kettering Town and he never will. But that champagne image is again part of the myth that he's happily let build up. Ron likes a drink now and again and likes to celebrate with champagne, but he doesn't take much of it himself. He's the sort who has one glass himself whilst going round continually topping up everyone else's. When the celebrations are over and four or five bottles have been drunk, Ron is still finishing off his one and only glass.

I think Ron is good for Manchester United because he is a big enough character to take on such a role. You couldn't have a shrinking violet running the team, because the City and the club demand a man of such quality and sparkle to keep them ahead. The pressure of doing well and keeping up with tradition at United is immense and it takes confidence to tackle such a role. I'm sure Ron Atkinson still has a lot to learn and a long future ahead of him, but he has the qualities and the skills to go down as one of the greats. One of the best things about Ron is that he can take a joke and relax when the pressure's not on. The best story about him came while we were with Albion. The team were down in London to play Arsenal and as usual we'd travelled down on the Friday night and stopped over. Saturday morning was spent relaxing and watching television and after a light lunch we all got together for the pre-match talk. Well the time of the meeting had been brought forward half an hour and the manager had sent the message to all the players. One chap who didn't get the message was winger Peter Barnes who was having a nap in his room. The Arsenal game was an important one for us and Ron had had them watched in order to give us a few clues on how to break them down. He went through the Arsenal team in detail and drew up the plans for the afternoon. As he outlined the tactics he eventually got to Peter Barnes' role. Well, Ron didn't realize that Peter wasn't in the room and spoke for about five minutes about what he wanted Peter to do. At the end of it he said 'OK Barnesy?' and looked around to get some acknowledgement from the England winger. All heads turned and we realized that the boss had been wasting his time.

'Where is he?' shouted Ron.

'He's upstairs having a lie down boss,' chirped Gary Owen the Albion midfielder, 'but don't worry too much, he never listens to you at team talks anyway!'

Some managers might have hit the roof at this stage, but Ron just burst out laughing and took it as a joke. Funnily enough the boy Barnes played a blinder that day and we had a great time pulling the manager's leg about it on the way home up the motorway.

On trips abroad Ron is always a good manager as well. He makes sure that training is seen to but also gives the players a fairly free hand to relax and enjoy themselves. I think his basic policy is that if we play well for him, he will look after us. Some managers are sticklers on players getting to bed on time before a big match and love to crack the whip. Ron is no soft touch, and anybody who's late for training will get a blasting, but he gives players their self-respect and makes them think and act for themselves. I know other managers criticize him for the way he attracts publicity. He's always got a word for every press man and even after the most disastrous of games I've seen Ron swallow his disappointment and face every question. His easy going manner makes him look at home. The players at United welcome this side of him, because a manager like Ron takes the pressure off us. Before a big match Ron will often come out with a special story so that all the pre-match publicity is focused on him. He can take it in his stride, allowing the players to slip into the background and prepare properly.

Before Ron arrived at Old Trafford there had been a procession of managers in recent years. Wilf McGuiness had a go before handing over the reins to Frank O'Farrell who inherited the problems George Best was posing at the time. After him came the irrepressible Tommy Docherty who, as usual, courted success and sensationalism. Dave Sexton, a quiet but clever man followed him, and next it was Ron Atkinson's turn. They all, of course, were trying to take over from Sir Matt Busby, the father of Manchester United. It was Sir Matt who, with his Busby Babes, had really built up United's world wide reputation. He took the club to five league championships, two Wembley FA Cup wins and in 1968 fulfilled his lifelong ambition of bringing the European Champion's Cup to England and Manchester for the first time. Sir Matt was Manchester United, and I'm sure all the managers who followed realized the standard they had to live up to. We only see him on match days at Old Trafford now, but he still takes great delight in talking to the players. He is a kind man, with a word of encouragement for everyone, and I only need to look around to realize what he achieved for the club. Without Sir Matt, United would not be the club it is today, and I often enjoy a chat with him. Talking to him, even these days, you realize what knowledge and love he has for the game, and in particular Manchester United. In his heyday, I bet he was quite a man, and as for the present United team, well he gives us all something to live up to, and aim for.

The first football manager I really got to know was Don Howe at West Bromwich. He'd been one of the Hawthorns' favourites as a player, and his coaching had helped

Arsenal to the double in the early seventies. But Don I think was never cut out to be a manager. When he was in charge at Albion, he seemed restless and let things get on top of him. The smallest problem would worry him, and this got through to the players who felt his unease. After quitting Albion, he went back to coaching, and finally settled back at Highbury, as well as helping out the England team. Don was not a good manager but he is a hell of a good coach. He's far more at ease now he's back in his real role, and I hope he never has the temptation to go back into management. To give some idea of how he's changed, Don hated his players having a drink when he was in charge at the Hawthorns, but now he'll think nothing of inviting you along for half a lager to discuss some aspect of the game. He gets accused of introducing boring tactics to the sport, which I think is unfair. Don is one of the finest coaches I've ever worked with and has a rare talent to help players. He'll work patiently on some move or part of your game in training over and over again until it's right and the England players rate 'The Don' very highly indeed.

Johnny Giles, who took over from him at Albion, was one of the best managers I've ever met. He had everything, and how sad it is his talents are not still with us in the first division. He was a brilliant player, a shrewd judge of a man and very down to earth. Even as a youngster I felt I could always take any problems to John Giles and he would go to any lengths to sort them out. Coaching wasn't perhaps one of his stronger points with young lads, but Giles was an immensely clever man who knew how to run a football club, and in his short stay with Albion proved how talented he was.

One of the greatest men I've ever come into contact with is the legendary Bill Shankly. I only wish I could have had the chance to play under him. After he left Anfield, he became friendly with Ron Atkinson, and used to lend some advice. Bill would quite often come to watch us play and when he did, Ron would invite him into the dressing room. I remember he came in before one game, and what impressed me was the way he went round the entire room, a word for every player. He was not one to deliver long sermons, they were little simple bits of advice. His manner and even his accent used to make me laugh and one of his great strengths was that he had the ability to tell a player off and crack a joke at the same time. Shankly could be scathing at times, but he chose his words so well players found themselves being torn off a strip and walking away with a broad grin on their face, instead of hanging their head low in despair. His successor at Liverpool, Bob Paisley, always struck me as a strange choice in so much as he was a very ordinary sort of chap for the position he was in. There is nothing fancy about him and you'd probably pass him in the street and not give him a second look. A very homely looking man, Paisley carries immense respect from every player in the game, purely for his record. Whenever we went to Anfield, Mr Paisley would always be most welcoming and was always the same cheery man in victory or defeat and I know the Liverpool lads had great respect for him.

One manager whom I admire more than most is Terry Venables, of Queens Park Rangers. Our paths first crossed with the England under-21 team, and straight away I was taken with his direct and sensible approach to everything. A very engaging and clever man, Venables is a manager who commands instant respect from his players. He knows exactly what he wants and doesn't beat about the bush. He's a fine coach as well, and must be one of the best all rounders in the game today. He's a very straightforward person who has many good ideas and plans for the game. You have only to look at the way he's developed Queens Park Rangers to make any judgement, and it would not surprise me to see Terry Venables running the England team one day. He has everything it takes and would be a popular choice among the players. Not that we want to get rid of Bobby Robson! He too is liked by all the England players, and without doubt was the best man for the job after Ron Greenwood.

Mr Robson is an easy man to get on with and draws the best out of his players. He was successful with Ipswich because he has certain ways and beliefs about football which he sticks by. I'm sure, given the chance, Bobby Robson will do a good job for the England team. His experience at all levels will prove invaluable to the national squad and he knows he has the backing of all the players. Bobby Robson, like Ron Greenwood, is more of a private man than say Ron Atkinson. When he's not coaching or dealing with the side he'll take himself away from the players. At first I thought he was something of a loner, but have discovered that's the way he likes to run his team. He's there when it counts, but doesn't want to smother us like a mother hen.

The man a lot of people put forward for the England job was Brian Clough. He's something of a mystery man to me, I've only met him at dinners and social functions, and we have always got on well. Without doubt he is a brilliant manager, and on occasions I think he is misunderstood. He has a mind of his own and just because he tends to go about life a little differently, he confuses some. How many managers, having taken their team to victory at Wembley, have gone home the same night, put the cup on the telly, and sat down with their family eating fish and chips? That was Cloughy after one of Forest's League Cup wins. I say good luck to him. Football needs men of his intelligence and style to make it tick, and I've always found him a very interesting man.

When I first met him I'd heard so much about him that I didn't know quite what to expect. He has a reputation for being an unpredictable and hard man. His bark, I reckon, might be worse than his bite, but I'm not sure whether I would like to play for him. From the tales I've heard from Forest players, Cloughy does some funny things at times, and he's not the sort of chap you can judge easily. I like to know where I am with managers, but I'm sure that, if you're straight and fair with Brian Clough then he would see you all right. Whether he would have made a good England manager though, is open to debate. He has skill and is capable of lifting the players around him. One of the things I admire in him most is the way he can get the best out of a player. It's all too easy for some managers to go out and keep buying player after player, and although Brian Clough has spent a few bob in his time on men such as Trevor Francis and Peter Shilton, he's also found a few like John Robertson, Garry Birtles and Tony Woodcock. Robertson was a nobody until Clough got hold of him, and look how he polished Woodcock, from being a reserve out on loan to Doncaster to an established English international. Clough is probably one of the best motivators in the game of football.

I don't think Brian Clough ever had a chance of getting the England job purely because his unpredictable style wouldn't go down well at Lancaster Gate. Although I believe in a man speaking his mind, I think Brian Clough can be his own worst enemy, by saying too much. There's a time to speak out and have a go, but there's also a time when you should sit and think and perhaps keep quiet. I don't think Cloughy would be diplomatic enough for an

England manager. But draw up a list of the top ten managers, and the name of Brian Clough would be battling for the top spot.

One encouraging development recently has been the way managers all over have been given more time to prove themselves. Football went through a crazy spell, when men were hired and fired with indecent haste if they didn't provide instant success. I'm sure many good men have been lost from football because they were so disillusioned by the way their livelihoods were whisked from under their feet by directors demanding results and nothing more. You only need to look at a club like Ipswich, Southampton or even Norwich to see that patience can often pay off. There are not many people who can walk into a football club, wave a magic wand and provide instant success. Every manager has his own style and should be allowed to show and develop it. It makes me angry when clubs take on a new manager and then panic after a run of disappointing results and give him the sack. It can take years to build a team, and if you want a job doing properly then it's worth spending a little time on making sure the foundations are firm.

I think that finance, or the lack of it, will bring out better managers in the seasons to come. The emphasis will be on finding and developing your own talent again, and I'm sure any manager will admit that he gets far more satisfaction from finding a young lad playing at school or local level and bringing him on to the first team, than opening up the cheque book. Will I go into management I wonder? Well, it's a natural progression for any player and one I've thought about. I must confess to no great ambitions in that line. As a lad I yearned to play for England and at Wembley, but have never had the same strong wish to run a club. I suppose I enjoy my game so much that I don't really want to think to a day when I'll have to hang up my boots. When that day comes, I may well try my hand as a manager, but I won't jump at the first opportunity that comes my way.

I think some players are so keen, or desperate in some cases, to get a job as a manager that they take the first chance that comes along. Quite often it can do them more harm than good. They find themselves in at the deep end, trying to save a sinking ship with a bucket full of holes. If, and when, I go looking for a manager's job, I'll take my time and try to find a club that suits me.

# 13
# *Matches to Remember*

When football fans or folk gather together their stories can be as tall as fishermen's, whose catches get longer and heavier every time they tell a story of how they landed a giant pike or sálmon. With the football followers it's players and matches they've been lucky enough to see.

What started off as a good shot from twenty yards ends up as a thunderbolt from thirty-five yards, wingers who beat a couple of defenders are made into wizards who left at least half a dozen in their wake. Time blurs the memory in most of us and I suppose it's a welcoming side of human nature that we usually manage to remember the good times more than the bad ones. It's the same in football. Players and fans can recall a memorable match kick by kick, while the nightmare games are quickly forgotten.

When I look back on my career as a player, there are many games that come to mind starting with a youth match for Albion across in Germany. I'll never forget it because I was only sixteen and it was in that match I first found form and discovered my confidence. It was the gateway to my career as a league footballer and after Germany I never looked back.

So far there have been four matches which will stay with me forever for different reasons. Two were with West Bromwich Albion, one with Manchester United and another with England. The first was in the UEFA Cup competition when Albion took on Valencia. We had made it to the third round of the competition with wins over the Turkish side Galatasaray and a second round triumph against Sporting Braga from Portugal. It was Albion's first season in Europe for ten years so for most of us in the team it was our first taste of continental football at club level. Valencia arrived in the third round having beaten the crack Bulgarian outfit CSKA Sofia and then the equally formidable Arges Pitesti from Rumania. But the lure of Valencia was the inclusion of two World Cup stars Mario Kempes and Rainer Bonhof in their side. Kempes had been one of the stars of the Argentine side which only a few months earlier had won the World Cup in Buenos Aires. In the final he scored two goals and was one of the most feared and respected players in world football. Bonhof had played for West Germany in the finals and was well worth his place in any World Eleven. So, the chance to play against these two excited and thrilled us all and as for me – what a challenge in midfield!

The first leg in front of fifty thousand people in Spain finished 1-1 with Laurie Cunningham getting the Albion equalizer in the second half. For Albion away from home it was a good result and we eagerly awaited the chance to get Valencia back on our own Hawthorns ground for the second leg. It was Wednesday December 6 1978 when we faced Valencia in that second leg. The town and its supporters had been looking forward to seeing the team play against Kempes and Bonhof. For days you could feel the excitement in the air, and a couple of hours before kick-off when we arrived at the ground large queues were building up.

This was the night when Albion's most promising team in years faced the real test. Victory would put us on the map, while defeat would see us lost with all the other also rans. A capacity crowd of nearly thirty-five thousand filled the Hawthorns and I can't ever remember getting such a warm welcome from the Albion fans as we ran out. The supporters around the Black Country enjoy their football but are by no means as devoted as those at Anfield or Old Trafford. But on this night they had done us proud and their cheers gave all the players the ideal lift for such an important match. With the scores level from the first leg we were the favourites to win but with players like Kempes and Bonhof facing us, we knew nothing could be taken for granted.

Valencia were desperate for victory to justify their large financial investment in two star players but after five minutes they found themselves in all sorts of trouble. Full-back Cordero handled as he went for a ball in front of his own goal and the referee gave a penalty to Albion. The Spanish side protested vehemently against the decision as their players surrounded the referee and even the manager jumped up and down on the touchline shaking his fists in the air with fury. But a penalty it was. Tony Brown confidently stepped up and despite the keeper moving too soon, his kick was well placed and tucked to the left to make it 1-0 to Albion. Valencia were still shaking with rage as they tried to get back into the game but five minutes after the penalty, it was Albion who suffered when Tony Brown got the ball in the net again, only to turn around and see the referee disallow the goal for a handball decision against Cyrille Regis, the Baggies centre-forward. This time it was our turn to protest but the referee was in a forceful mood and there was clearly no point in wasting time and energy arguing with him. We had also been lectured by manager Ron Atkinson about the danger of getting too involved in arguments with Spanish sides. Along with the Italians, the Spanish have a habit of trying to destroy your concentration with niggling fouls, arguments or feigning injury. No end of British clubs have fallen for these tricks but we were determined to steer clear of them.

At half-time Albion still led from the penalty, but three minutes into the second half we were denied again by another strange decision from the referee. In the dressing room at half-time we'd agreed that an early goal would kill the Valencia fightback, so out we went with all guns firing to score. And when full-back Derek Statham hit the back of the net we all turned to celebrate only to see the referee blowing for offside against me. It was one of the oddest decisions I've ever witnessed and for a moment I think one or two of the Albion players began to worry. Was the tide of fortune beginning to flow against us? Was it going to be one of those nights when fate ruled us out? Those thoughts were strengthened a few minutes later when Laurie Cunningham had a header which hit the foot of the Valencia post. To make matters worse the Spaniards were beginning to find their form. Kempes swerved a free kick around the Albion wall, to have it palmed away by keeper Tony Godden. A few moments later Kempes again carved us open with a beautiful pass which found substitute Diarte. Fortunately his shot went wide, but the warning bells were beginning to ring. Kempes was on the march. He hadn't had the best of games in the first half, and we watched him closely but his ability was such that one pass, one turn, or one shot could change everything.

Bonhof luckily was below par but what a test it was to stop Kempes from taking over in midfield. It was a battle we won with the reliable Tony Brown making sure of victory with just eleven minutes to go. Laurie Cunningham floated past Cordero as though the full-back wasn't there and his cross was met with a tremendous volley by Bomber Brown. It was a goal from the minute it left his boot and the cheer as it smacked against the back of the net rocked the West Midlands. Valencia, Kempes and all were finished and West Bromwich Albion had slain one of the most respected and talented sides in Europe. It was a great battle to win and a memorable game to play in. For me it was one of the most satisfying results of my career and the next day we were hailed by the press as El Magnifico.

My second great game came a couple of weeks later at Old Trafford. Albion went to Manchester without having had a win against United there in nineteen years. It was the Saturday between Christmas and New Year, so everyone was in the festive spirit, and against Valencia and United the Albion team reached its peak. I suppose that's why these two matches have stayed with me. The Albion team then was the best I ever played in at the Hawthorns, and after December we never recaptured the same form. The sparkle went and at the end of the season the side began to break up. But what memories of Old Trafford I have, when for once I took great delight in seeing the mighty Manchester United thrashed. Manager Ron Atkinson described the game as the best he'd ever seen in the first division, and it's a match that any true Albion fan will, to this day, be able to relate to you kick by kick.

In the run up to facing United we had dropped just two points in ten matches and were chasing Liverpool and Everton for top spot. Although we started well against United it was they who took the lead after about twenty minutes when Brian Greenhoff scored with a spectacular volley. They were only in front though for five minutes because Cunningham set up the equalizer for Tony Brown and that goal lit the fuse. A minute later Len Cantello, who was having a great day in midfield, scored with a thundering shot from twenty yards, which scorched into the United net; we were 2-1, but within seconds United were back for the equalizer. A free kick from Stewart Houston was met with a firm header from Gordon

McQueen, a giant of a man, and with four goals inside twenty-eight minutes Old Trafford was shaking with excitement. It was one of the fastest and most enjoyable games I've ever played in. With so many goals early on both teams threw down the gauntlet to each other and it really was cut and thrust. I know that in midfield I didn't dare stop to catch breath for fear of those red shirts sweeping up for another goal, but four minutes later they took the lead again when Sammy McIlroy skilfully worked his way through the Albion defence to score. It was a marvellous goal, and for a few moments we found ourselves struggling to get back in the game. But right on half time Derek Statham found Cantello in the box. His header was knocked down to Tony Brown who nudged the ball past Gary Bailey to make it 3-3. The equalizer could not have come at a better time, nor could the referee's whistle for half-time. I felt as though I'd just run a marathon in half an hour. My lungs were tightening and my head buzzing as I made for the dressing rooms and a much needed rest. Not much was said during the break because no one had enough breath to say anything, but the goal on half-time had lifted us enormously and running back out for the second half we knew we could win it. 1978 had been a good year for all of us, and what better way to finish it off than with a victory at Old Trafford.

The game was ours for much of the second half. United were struggling under the pressure of Cunningham's runs down the wing and in the middle Cyrille Regis was causing all sorts of problems for McQueen and Martin Buchan. Gary Bailey pulled off some remarkable saves in goal and one goalbound effort was cleared off the line by Brian Greenhoff. Eventually we got the breakthrough. A long clearance from Tony Godden was helped on by Regis to Cunningham. His speed was such that the United defenders were made to look as though they were standing still as Cunningham sprinted towards goal like a cheetah after his prey. He scored with a controlled low drive which found the corner of the net. Cunningham at his best was worth travelling a long way to watch, and never again did I see him play so brilliantly. His control of the ball while he was running as fast as a sprinter for the tapes was his greatest quality, and if not for injury Laurie Cunningham would surely have been one of the England greats. With five minutes to go Regis finished United off when he pounced to ram the ball home and Albion had won 5-3.

Apart from the crowd of just over forty-five thousand, millions more were able to enjoy the game on television. I watched it over and over again, and even today thanks to the wonder of the video age hundreds of Albion fans relive those goals. If that team had stayed together, the league championship trophy would have come to the Hawthorns. Only in recent months with the emergence of the new look Manchester United have I played with such a strong all round team. The eleven men that flattened United in December 1978 were Godden, Batson, Statham, Tony Brown, Wile and Robertson, myself, Ally Brown, Regis, Cantello and Cunningham. If an Albion fan ever asked me to name my all-time team for the Hawthorns I wouldn't need to think twice – the eleven that beat Valencia and Manchester United would be it.

I think it will be hard to match that game for enjoyment from a team's point of view, but my third memorable match gave me a great personal satisfaction. It was for England against France in Bilbao in the summer of 1982 at the start of the World Cup. With England having scraped through to the finals everyone was prepared to write us off and the France game was a tough one with which to start.

The French were a useful side with players such as Platini to watch out for. With the temperature up in the nineties walking out for the start of the World Cup was like stepping into a fire. The match had been built up for weeks and we all knew we desperately needed a victory against France to stand any chance of doing well in the later stages.

For me the game couldn't have started better. From the kick-off we worked the ball straight up field and I ran into space for a cross which I met perfectly by stretching out my left foot. Before I realized it the ball was in the back of the net and the goal had come so quickly that even the England fans had been stunned into silence by the speed of it all. It was a peculiar feeling seeing the ball in the net so quickly. For a few seconds the world stopped and fell silent as I turned to celebrate. There was such a look of utter disbelief on the French faces that I had to look back at the goal and then at the referee to make sure I'd scored. The goal was officially timed at twenty-seven seconds. The fastest goal in the history of the World Cup Finals and everywhere I go the memory of that goal stays with me. As a reward for being the fastest goalscorer in a match in Spain, sponsors had offered a solid gold watch, and that goal against France won it for me. So whenever I look for the time on my watch there's the memory of that goal.

Our celebrations were not all that long lived because France gradually steered themselves back in the game. Alain Giresse was their star. He was in brilliant form and a long pass from him found Soler in the twenty-fifth minute who beat Peter Shilton to make it 1-1. Alongside Giresse, Platini was beginning to hit form and as we approached half-time I must admit that our chances of winning were declining. The French were beginning to dictate the game from midfield and the England defence,

Kenny Sansom apart, were having a harrowing time. The half-time whistle was a relief and during the break Ron Greenwood tried to build us up and convince us we could still beat the French. Graham Rix dropped back into a more defensive role and in the second half we came alive. Trevor Francis came out of his shell and played some of his best football, turning and testing the French defence at every opportunity. Paul Mariner looked as sharp as I've ever seen him for England and Steve Coppell ran and ran. It was one of the most stirring England comebacks I've ever experienced and the French were taken aback by our new found confidence.

Midway through the second half we got the second goal. Francis darted down the right and sent in a wonderfully flighted cross. I was running in and could see the French were hesitating. I knew that if I could get there I could score and with about ten feet to make up I threw myself forward and met the ball crisply with my head. England 2 France 1 and before they had a chance to settle Rix, Wilkins and Francis combined to create a chance for Paul Mariner to make it 3-1 and England's World Cup campaign was well underway. After the match I can remember telling reporters that the two goals were the best I'd ever scored and what gave me such satisfaction was that I'd managed to play well in a World Cup tournament. Before the Finals people talked of me as a potential player of world class and I felt the pressure was on me to prove I had the ability to live with the best. The World Cup provides the ideal stage for a footballer, just look at what Wembley in 1966 did for the England team. One minute they were just internationals, the next they were world class players.

After that France game I felt that for the first time I had made my mark for England. I suppose every game you play for your country is one to treasure and I only hope that before I finish my football career I have the opportunity to surpass the France game with a World Cup Final . . .

My fourth and last great game came for Manchester United in the 1983 FA Cup Competition. It might surprise you that I enjoyed the semi-final against Arsenal at Villa Park in Birmingham more than the actual final or replay against Brighton at Wembley Stadium. Why? Well because the Arsenal match was a bigger hurdle for us and there's an immense satisfaction in getting to Wembley. Losing a semi-final is the worst feeling of all, so perhaps winning one is the best. The Arsenal game I remember well because it represented a dramatic comeback by United which took tremendous team work and courage. Going into the semi-final our season rested on this one game. If we had lost then our year would have been fruitless but victory would take us to Wembley and a Cup Final. We had already beaten Arsenal in the semi-final of the Milk Cup and at this stage there was a great deal of rivalry between us. United were the favourites to win but any side that carries the symbol of the Arsenal canon can never be discounted.

Having badly injured my ankle against Arsenal in the home leg of our Milk Cup semi-final the Villa Park match was only my second after being carried off. The first thirty minutes were everything you'd expect in a semi-final. Every ball had to be fought for and both teams were tense with the fear of making a mistake. Arsenal took the lead with only nine minutes to go to half-time. A cross to the far post for some reason caused panic in our goalmouth. Gary Bailey tried to get hold of it but failed and eventually Tony Woodcock poked the ball home. The goal left us cold and we could have been sunk there and then if

Arsenal had really gone for us. As we started the second half we all knew how badly we needed a goal, and Arsenal with one foot on Wembley Way had to be cracked open. With just four minutes gone Ashley Grimes sent a ball to me on the edge of the box. I knew Brian Talbot was on my heels so I turned as quickly as I could, steering the ball past Talbot and then brought my left foot across my body to pull the ball wide of George Wood in the Arsenal goal for the equalizer. That was the breakthrough we needed. We knew then we could reach Wembley and I suspect that Arsenal, although far from surrendering, were beginning to come to the same conclusion.

We piled on the pressure and Arsenal finally gave in after seventy minutes when Norman Whiteside ran in behind the Gunners' defence to volley home. That semi-final was one of the closest games I've ever played in and to come back from behind and win always gives a side immense satisfaction, especially in a cup semi-final when first blood can be so vitally important. The Arsenal semi-final was a true test of the character and grit of the United team. Having good players or talented individuals is all very well but you also need a team of fighters to achieve success in football and that sunny April day at Villa Park we proved there was more to Manchester United than its glorious tradition.

I hope that in five or six years time I can look back with such satisfaction and recall some more great games, but now from the sublime to the ridiculous – the only match I can ever remember not enjoying, a game for Albion against Leicester City at Filbert Street. We lost 2-1 and I was so bad that I was substituted in the second half. When it comes to spinning a few stories for the grandchildren I think I'll settle for Albion against the dashing Valencia, or how Albion blasted five past Manchester United at Old

Trafford, the twenty-seven-second goal which stunned the French or the battle of Villa Park which took Manchester United to a Wembley Final. It's true you know, the more you tell them . . . the better they get!

# 14

## *Something Must be Done*

When George Orwell wrote of 1984 it must have scared the living daylights out of people all those years ago. And although Big Brother hasn't taken over yet, it's a year which could still go down forever in history – as the one in which football died, or started to breathe new life.

Since the seventies football has been in trouble. Hooligans have run riot on the terraces; television has given the game more exposure; clubs have spent more money than ever on players; players have won freedom of contract and the economic crisis has bitten more into life.

When I was a kid in Chester-le-Street, football was a way of life. Everybody, young or old had a team. In our town it was either Sunderland or Newcastle. Not everyone went to cheer their heroes on, but crowds of well over forty thousand were the average at St James Park or Roker.

The north east has always been a great breeding ground for footballers and supporters alike, so the fervour there was incredibly strong. When I moved to the Midlands I noticed that football was not quite as important, but even there everyone had a team whether it be Albion, Villa, Wolves or Birmingham. After the weather, football used to be the one subject that would be guaranteed to break the ice on a long train or bus journey. It was the country's national sport and nobody played football like the Brits. In the fifties and early sixties the European travels of Manchester United and Wolves did much to foster international relations and if one thing could unite the world it was sport, and more often than not football.

Even the Iron Curtain was no barrier to football and was it not West Bromwich Albion which became one of the first teams of sportsmen to be invited into China? Back in the fifties Manchester United would have crowds of sixty and seventy thousand nearly every week, whether the opposition be Manchester City or Burnley. The nation loved its football and Saturday afternoon was the time when dad would take his family or young lad to watch the local team. Those days have sadly long gone. They don't queue any more and the game is facing its biggest ever dilemma. When I was a lad a crowd of around twenty-three or twenty-four thousand at a football match was a poor gate . . . nowadays it's a good one. Every season the attendances have sunk and I know there are those who predict that football is dying.

The question is can the disease which is eating it away be operated on or is it incurable? Will 1984 see football given its last rites? Some blame the fans, some the players, some the clubs, some the administrators and some the media. Surely they are all to blame in one way or another and can all help make the game healthy and put it back on its feet.

First the fans. Violence on the terraces has been one of football's biggest problems and there must be thousands who have been frightened off by the mindless thuggery of youngsters who dare to call themselves football supporters. Manchester United has had more than its share of problems with unruly fans as a trail of wreckage left up and down the country has proved. I don't honestly think I'd let a child of mine go to a football match on their own if they were older for fear of their being harmed. But is crowd violence just down to football? Surely it is a symptom of a society that is growing more violent by the day. My argument on football violence is this. If rugby union or cricket were the most popular spectator sport before football, would not the fans transfer their allegiance and violence to those? In the fifties there were Teddy boys, in the early sixties mods and rockers and after that came the football rowdies.

Apart from one or two incidents football violence has not been so great over the past few years. The youngsters who travel the country looking for fights and trouble at football grounds are not real supporters. If all football stopped tomorrow, you would still get gangs fighting against one another. Instead of on the terraces though, they'd probably do battle in the local disco or park.

To the players there is nothing more sickening than seeing violence in the crowd. We play for the people, it's their game to be enjoyed, not an excuse for gang warfare. The short-term solution on crowd violence is to make the penalties harsher. But before the fingers of blame are all pointed in the direction of local football clubs wouldn't it be worth taking a closer look at some of the backgrounds these troublemakers come from?

At our school in Chester-le-Street the cane was used as a deterrent. A few lashes of that were enough to make anyone behave. I know I used to fear getting into trouble and being ordered to the headmaster's study for a few strokes of the big stick. I was caned once for being sent off in a football match of all things, but that was the first and last time. I don't think it did me any harm. What it did do was to teach me respect and how to behave myself. So I think an overall decline in the standards of discipline has much to do with the football violence we've had in the last ten years or so.

Next the players. We have been accused of bleeding the game dry with demands for large amounts of money and long contracts. In the forties and fifties many footballers lived on the breadline. The sixties, with the pioneering work of Jimmy Hill, brought an end to the maximum wage and gradually from there Freedom of Contract evolved. As a player I thought Freedom of Contract was designed to give us more choice and the chance to live a more normal life. Before Freedom of Contract a player was tied to his club and once he had signed for them, even when his contract ran out, there could be a long fight to move away. New rules meant that once a player had served his contract he could, like most people, decide to move elsewhere to another job, or in his case to a different club.

What happened was unfortunate. Clubs panicked about losing their best players and tried to beat Freedom of Contract by offering long and lucrative new agreements. Players found themselves being asked to sign on for anything from six to eight years and in return were offered staggering wages. The result was that many clubs overstretched themselves financially and before very long were in trouble. Bristol City was one club which having given long contracts to its players, discovered later when they were relegated from the first division that they could not afford to keep going at that pace. Clubs feared the Freedom of Contract instead of trying to understand it and work within it. What clubs should have done is to have taken a firmer grip and been harder on the players. People were quick to blame the players, but it was the clubs which were offering vast amounts of money, thinking they could buy success. Now, thankfully, after the initial confusion of Freedom of Contract, the transfer market and players' wages have levelled out. The good players are paid well as in any other sport, but they realize they can't hold clubs to ransom. And by the same token, clubs have at last taken a stand realizing they must be prepared to reward well for talent but don't have to pay over the odds because none of their rivals will either.

Another train of thought is that interest in football has dwindled and crowds have dropped because the average player has moved away from the supporters. Years ago footballers earned as much as office clerks and lived around the corner on the local housing estate. As wages have risen, so have living standards and nowadays most first division men can afford to move out to the more expensive areas. But I don't really see this argument has any foundation. Both at Albion and at United the players went out of their way to keep in close contact with the supporters' clubs, by attending social evenings or dances. When you look at other sports the fact that Jack Nicklaus is a millionaire and lives in a luxury home has no effect surely on his pulling power with the followers of golf? The footballer's life has changed, but when we are accused of earning too much money it's worth taking a look at other sports. Success in tennis, golf, boxing or even snooker can bring far greater rewards.

Another factor that's been blamed for the alarming drop in football attendances is television. I think TV plays a strange role in football. It can be its best friend or alternatively its worst enemy. Too much football on television, I think, does have some effect on gates. There was a time when you could sit down over the weekend and watch just about every goal scored in the first division. And on a typical wet and windy day, a warm armchair in front of the telly has to be more welcoming than some draughty old football stand. So, too much telly can affect football. But on the other hand, the sport needs publicity. If only a few games are shown, then it will surely whet the appetite for people to get up out of their chairs and go to the local ground and watch. The dominance of television and to some less extent radio and newspapers has taken away the thrill of being there for the average football fan. When we were kids, actually being there at St James Park when Wyn Davies cracked home a hat-trick was unbeatable. It was something to be able to turn round and say of a great match . . . 'I saw it, I was there.' Nowadays people can turn around and say 'Oh well, I saw it on the telly, heard it on the radio or read about it in the newspapers.' It's vital that football rekindles its dying flame and shows supporters once more that there is something worth watching.

Those are the problems, where on earth do we look for the solutions? In my mind, only one thing can save football and that is the creation of a 'super league'. If something is not done within the next year or two then football will surely die. A super league of sixteen teams together with a first division and a second division and then linked to regional leagues would give football a new dimension. With sides now allowed to keep all of their gate receipts, the rich are only going to get richer and the poor poorer, so a super league has to be the answer. With only sixteen teams in the league it would mean that less games would be played. This would have quite an effect on the standard of football. At the moment we play far too much. For the successful sides there are league matches, Milk Cup matches, the FA Cup and then European ties. On top of that, International games appear in midweek. Add those together and from the middle of August to the end of May it's one long slog.

I think that the amount of games we have to play in this country lowers the standard of football for two major reasons. First of all there is no time between matches for sides to really work on their game. If more time was spent on developing skills and moves in the week, then surely the football would be brighter at the weekend. The second reason is that at the moment far too many players are forced to run out and give everything they have when they're not really fit. I wouldn't like to count the number of times I've had to play carrying an injury. A leg strain or pulled muscle can be strapped up, but with less matches the players would have time to recover between games and when it came to the next match would be fully fit again. If the standard of football improved then it would attract more people back through the turnstiles to watch. And with only sixteen teams in a super league there would be less matches for them to see, which means they could afford to go to more of the games. These days people pick and choose which match they want to watch but with a super league every game, in theory, would be a good one.

The first division and second division could also be reduced in size to around sixteen teams each, and here again, less matches should produce brighter football. Some might say that the super league would kill off some of the smaller clubs, but sooner or later it must be realized that football will become the survival of the fittest. The first and second division with promotion and relegation could still prosper. The third and fourth division could join forces with the major non-league clubs and start a set of regional leagues. This would have to be part-time because I don't think that towns like Crewe and Stockport can really afford to keep a professional team going. But what's wrong with a thriving part-time club? Look at Runcorn, Altrincham and Scarborough and see the strides they have taken over the years. Some are better off than third and fourth division teams. Playing regional football would also reduce the overheads and there would be an even sounder base for youngsters wanting to come into the game.

At the moment there is a great divide between amateur or non-league football and the professional level. If the third and fourth divisions went part-time there would be less of a gap and more players would be given the chance to prove themselves at a higher level. All the teams could be linked by the FA Cup which still manages to capture the imagination – when the Manchester Uniteds and Liverpools find themselves up against the likes of Harlow or Bishops Stortford.

The Milk Cup could be fought out between the first, second and regional league sides leaving the teams in the super league time to concentrate on playing in the European competitions. Another great advantage of a super league system would be that less games would also help international teams. Every national manager has complained in the past of his plans being hit by injuries. When England have a midweek game the players only get together on the Sunday before. Some spend two days shaking off a knock or a strain, while the others try to get used to playing alongside each other again. If the game is away, then by the time the squad has travelled to their destination, it's usually Tuesday before training gets underway. With a super league and fewer matches the national team managers would have more time in which to get their players together and the result, hopefully, would be a healthier and more successful team.

Another important area football has to take a close look at is treating the supporters properly. At the moment, a lot of our football grounds are a disgrace. Most are old and in a poor state of repair, offering the fans little or no facilities. On a cold wet afternoon, the local stadiums hardly look inviting. On the terraces you have to endure the worst of weather and put up with the obscene language that is often heard or chanted. Some of the stands can be as bad as you sit crammed in, your knees pressed against your chest on a rock-hard seat. The catering facilities are a joke. Quite often you can't tell the difference between a cup of tea or a mug of Bovril. The hot pies are often lukewarm and the sandwiches like lumps of rubber. The food and drink aren't cheap either, and the chap on the terrace must feel some resentment when he looks towards the executive boxes and sees others wining and dining in style. And why shouldn't he be given better treatment? I think all grounds in the country should go all-seated. Coventry City, I know, experimented with this and were not too happy with the results, but I think if all clubs were made to go all-seated the fans would soon adjust. I can hear the outcry from the Stretford End or Liverpool's Kop, that the atmosphere and part of the tradition of football would be ruined, but sooner or later the game has to change its image. We can't afford to live in the past forever. All-seater stadiums would offer more comfort for the fans and I think that at the same time it might help tackle the threat of crowd violence. Clubs should also be made to spend more money on their grounds by way of improving the other facilities. There should be comfortable cafeterias with good food served instead of greasy snack bars. Why not amusement rooms with space invader machines, or television lounges where people could relax in some style before and after the game?

I'm a great believer in the American sporting way. Over in the States, the paying public are treated like guests, not as cattle. A trip to an American football game or a baseball match is a family day out. They can be assured of a comfortable seat, of a tasty and reasonably priced snack, and of entertainment. A super league would hopefully provide more entertaining football and if only clubs improved their facilities then surely more would come back to watch. In the past too many football clubs have been guilty of neglecting their supporters. They've tended to take them for granted. But now with family sports like basketball and badminton gaining in popularity, I think the message is at last beginning to hit home.

Over the last few years a lot of time and money has been spent on attracting big business into the game, by providing executive lounges and splendidly appointed glass fronted boxes around the ground. That's a good idea because football does need money and sponsorship from business to keep it going, but it's time now that the supporters were treated better. I realize many clubs are in a difficult position because they're tied to grounds which were built in the early twenties. Many are squashed in between houses and factories, leaving little room for re-development or modernization. But instead of the annual lick of paint during the summer, they should seriously think about making changes. Money put aside for buying players could even be used. After all if the supporters are persuaded to come back through the turnstiles, more money will be generated and some of that could be used for transfers. Another important factor for the future is that football gets closer to its public. As I've mentioned players are happy to help out supporters' clubs by attending social evenings and special events, but more than that is called for. A football ground should be more than a stadium used once a week for three or four hours. Facilities like sports halls and clubs should be added to ensure that it serves the local people. Besides, the main exercise is to get supporters used to going to their local club, either for a game of squash in the sports hall, or for a pint and a bite to eat in the club. Several teams have already started joining up with developers to offer more than a football stadium.

Queens Park Rangers have of course put in artificial turf. I know this has great advantages, in that the ground can be used for many other purposes such as concerts, but I think football as we know it belongs on grass and I wouldn't like to see too many artificial pitches. When clubs plan for the future, they might be able to put in an all-weather pitch for training on . . . that's a cracking idea because it could be used by local teams or schools in the afternoon instead of standing idle.

The future of football has been a strong talking point for years now. Committees have been formed to look ahead into the crystal ball, and weighty reports have been drawn up. Nine out of ten have been put on the shelf to gather dust as the crisis deepens.

On behalf of the players I would like to appeal to the clubs along with the Football Association and Football League to make some drastic decisions in 1984. This should be the year of change. The year when football makes the break from its traditions. Supporters should be made to feel welcome and a super league formed. If nothing is done, then in ten or twenty years football will be an ailing, minority sport.

# 15

## *Tips to Reach the Top*

You've got to think high to rise
You've got to be sure of yourself before
You can ever win a prize
Life's battles don't always go
To the stronger or faster man
But sooner or later the man who wins
Is the one who thinks he can.

Football and poetry are not usually thought of as being similar but in those seven lines of striking verse, which sadly were written by an unknown pen, lies the best advice for any young footballer. As captain of England and Manchester United I am always asked when I meet kids at schools or clubs 'How do you make it to the top in football?' Hard work, dedication and skill are three obvious words which trip off the tongue, but perhaps the most important is determination. The will to win can take you far in football, as in any other sport, and it's something you need from the very start.

Millions of young boys dream of becoming professional footballers. In the early days their ambitions are confined to the back garden where every ball kicked against the wall or fence is either a defence splitting pass for England in a vital World Cup game or a breathtaking last minute goal for their team in a Wembley Cup Final. Next comes the chance to play for a school team or youth club side where at first it's kick and run. The game is like the hunt after a fox . . . twenty skinny lads chasing and racing after the ball. Then comes the senior school football. The ballplayers begin to emerge as they demonstrate their skills against the big, physical runners. For the lucky ones the chance arises to go further. County or district teams and then on the horizon the lure of the league clubs. Tests and trials are next with a few making their way on to the first step as an apprentice. But from the word go it's determination that can drive you on. I'm convinced there are hundreds, if not thousands of players, who if only they had been given more guidance or coaching and had more determination would have played professional football.

Some people are obviously born with skill or a gift for football, but there are many more who start on the same level as everybody else. In my case I was brought up to love and appreciate the game but when I first joined West Bromwich Albion there were times when I wondered if I'd ever make it any further. My weight problem was always the main worry and after a few months my confidence began to sag. But looking around I knew in my own mind that I was good enough to make the grade and so strong was my determination to play in league football that I would go back after morning training at the Hawthorns to work on my own. If I'd sat back and not fought to build myself up and improve my game then no doubt I would have been cast by the wayside. Thousands of young boys aim to be footballers but only a very small percentage actually make it. So how do they manage it?

One of the most important factors in the early days is to have a teacher or coach who takes an interest and drives you on. I was lucky in so much that Bill Chapman, my school soccer teacher, was passionate about the game and knew how it should be played. He gave up hours of his spare time to help those lads who shared his love of football by arranging extra training sessions either out on the field or in the gym. He would go to great lengths to make sure you were doing everything right and was always full of encouragement. But he was also quick to point out your mistakes or weaknesses. I know that in some crowded schools there is a danger of the teacher just throwing the ball to a group of lads and leaving them to their own devices or in some cases I'm sure the games period falls on the shoulders of someone who is not that well versed in the game. Bill Chapman was a teacher who had time for everyone who wanted to listen, and he set about his coaching very simply. The first step was to make sure all the lads could tackle the basics, such as kicking with both feet and heading, and he would make us practise the simple things over and over again until they became second nature.

It makes me laugh when so called soccer experts go to great lengths to talk about coaching and tactics when football can be, and should be, such a simple game. Young lads need encouragement more than anything else when they start playing and should just concentrate on the simple things. Whether they play 4 4 2 or 4 3 3 is immaterial to nine or ten year olds. They should learn how to kick and pass straight, how to control the ball and to enjoy themselves. A football career is like building a house. Not enough time can be spent on the foundations, but if you rush those, then later on cracks will begin to appear in your game. You can practise by knocking a ball against the wall or if there's a group of you passing it to each other. These simple exercises help your accuracy and control, and the more you do the better the feel of the ball you can get. When the basics are learnt it's then time to worry more about the game, your team mates and on occasions the opposition.

I think in the early stages it's very important that youngsters are encouraged to create their own style and be allowed to express it. There's a danger when lads get into their early teens of them being overcoached and made something they are not. In youth football freedom is important and players should not be shackled with worries of who to mark or how much space should be covered. They should be encouraged to play the game openly and build on their own skills. It is a good idea for youngsters to watch and perhaps study their favourite players but a mistake that's often made is to copy. Each and every player should have his own way of playing and it's important we encourage this. Coaches tend to churn out stereotyped players, but it's worth remembering that scouts always have an eye for a player who does something a little bit different or who shows some creativity.

When boys reach their mid-teens the more intensive training can start. One of the first things is to learn how to play in, and with the rest of the team. That might sound a bit strange, but it's only natural for young players to be selfish with the ball, after all when you are ten or eleven everyone wants to score a goal. Ball watching is one of the commonest complaints. I know it's easy to stand and watch one of your team mates go charging down the field, and then when he's stuck in a corner or faces a wall of opposing defenders he turns and cries for help. You have to learn to run with him, or for him. By running with him you are always there for the pass or by running for him you can perhaps make space to receive the ball further up field. Alternatively you can distract the opposition by running in between them and they'll be forced to keep an eye on you as well as the man with the ball. It's all very basic knowledge but it's amazing how many kids are not told about this side of the game before it's too late. Another piece of golden advice I was given at school was to let the ball do the work. If you watch any league side most of the passes are made up of short, straightforward balls. Young lads tend to try to kick the ball too hard and too far. Instead why not pass it a few yards? You won't need as much power and there's a better chance of the pass being on target.

It's also vital that kids are shown how to watch what they are doing. By that I mean to be able to look up and see what's going on around them and which players are free to pass to, or if it's clear, to line up a shot on goal. Youngsters naturally play with their heads down at first as they charge into battle with the ball at their feet. But if they know the basics they should be confident enough to be able to look up and still have control of the ball. Vision is so important in football and to a budding player can make all the difference between making the grade or dropping out. As in chess or any other tactical game you should always be thinking of the next move or pass and asking yourself what will my opponent do if I do that? On the football field of course that decision has to be made in a split second and in the end is down to instinct . . . which comes from training and preparing the proper way. These are all simple tips but I feel important ones to youngsters who want to be footballers.

One of the golden rules in the game is that you can never learn enough or be fit enough. I don't pretend, nor I'm sure does any other professional come to that, to know everything about football. Even today I am learning new things by experience or discovering different ways of approaching problems. I suppose when you are playing for your country it's automatically assumed that you know everything there is to know, but a good example of this is, as I said earlier, when Terry McDermott, who was then with Liverpool, took me aside after one England training session and advised me to vary my shots at goal more. It was a short and simple piece of advice but it made an awful lot of difference to my goalscoring.

Another important factor is fitness and training. I've always been a great believer in training hard and keeping yourself in good condition. This is where I differ with some experts on the game when it comes to players such as Alan Hudson, Charlie George, Stan Bowles and more recently Glen Hoddle. Now all of these have been rightly labelled as great artists, skilled ball players and craftsmen. The train of thought was that if Alan Hudson made some brilliant passes then it didn't matter too much if he didn't run back and help the defence out or make a larger contribution to the game. The English footballer is sometimes criticized for being too physical but I think that Hudson, Bowles, George and co. would have been better players if they had been made to work harder. Glen Hoddle is the best example. When he first came into the England team he carried with him a reputation for being a gifted player. When he was on form he was brilliant, but on his off days would disappear. In recent months Glen has worked harder on his contribution and involvement in the game and now when he plays for England works harder than he's ever done before. The result has been astonishing. Glen's natural ability has been complemented by his extra work rate or output and in my opinion he's a more complete player now he's changed, than he was when he first emerged as an England international.

Another prime example is the Brazilian team. They have always been regarded as the best in the world, and been held up as the example. Their skill is astonishing, but next time you watch Brazil study how much effort they put into a game. It's not just a question of them floating around delivering clever passes and flicks. The Brazilians buzz with work. They never stop running and working for each other, and this is often forgotten. We should encourage talented players, but at the same time there is no substitute for sheer hard work. I'm convinced that Stan Bowles say, would have been twice the player he was if along the way someone had got hold of him and made him work harder. Coaches tend to excuse players with ability from working too hard and yet it's a shame that more don't realize that in such players there is even more untapped talent waiting to be used up. From my schooldays when Bill Chapman took an interest, training has always been very important. For young lads any sort of training or practice should be made enjoyable rather than the spoonful of nasty medicine that has to be gulped down.

There are professional players I know who hate too much hard physical running or exercising in training and yet it can make all the difference. I'm often asked about my own fitness because some people think I've got some secret recipe for running harder and faster than a lot of people. I think it goes back to my teens when I was smaller and lighter than most of my friends. It was made clear by West Bromwich Albion that unless I grew taller and put on weight I'd never make it as a footballer no matter how good I was. Apart from special diets I did an awful lot of training. Running to build up stamina and weightlifting to make the muscles stronger. Back at home, Bill Chapman devised a special training programme and we would work together on it. It was hard at first and there were times when determination alone drove me on but the weights and exercises improved my build and gave me extra strength. A lot of coaches nowadays rightly put fitness behind skill and ball craft but to any young player it's vital that he prepares well and keeps himself extremely fit. If you look on the parks on a Sunday you'll see it's the fitter players that catch the eye and even in the first division it's surprising the difference an extra inch of pace can make. I think the secret to fitness is to work hard early on and then make sure you never let go of it. At the start of the season all players have to work a little harder to build up their fitness after the summer break, but then it's just a question of keeping yourself ticking over.

Regular training also means you can lead a more normal life style and not worry too much about putting on weight. The odd meal out or a couple of beers can easily be worked off in training the following morning and that's where the non-league or amateur players suffer. Their training is probably restricted to a couple of nights a week and it's a lot harder to work off three days extra food or drink.

Another useful tip I was given at the start was to listen to all advice, whether you take heed of it or not is another thing. There has not been a player in the history of the game who's known everything and football is a sport in which hundreds of people will try to tell you what's right and wrong. But if you don't listen to advice as a player then you'll be much poorer. There are those within the game who seem to think that it's only people who have actually played at the highest level who know what they are talking about. That's not always the case, because sometimes you can gain useful advice from outside the game. My Dad has always followed me closely of course, and although he never played the game at professional level, his knowledge of football spreads back many years. He still offers advice and it's always welcome. The same with my teacher Bill Chapman. He too was not a professional footballer, but experience counts for a lot, and without his advice in those days at school I might not have made it.

Another important lesson for a budding footballer to learn is one of discipline. The present system where lads are signed on as apprentices is I believe a good one because it helps to teach them a code of conduct. I know that when I was with the Albion as a sixteen-year-old the daily chores were sometimes most unpleasant. Sweeping out dressing rooms, cleaning boots until your hands ached and collecting up dirty, smelly kit was not my idea of being a professional footballer and I can see the same look on some of the young apprentices at United. You sign for a club to play football, not to act as cleaner and odd job boy. But looking back, it taught me to respect people and I think prepared me well for the later stages. There was never any possibility of apprentice players becoming too big headed at the Hawthorns, because those that went round shooting their mouths off or showing off were knocked down to size by being given a bigger list of jobs the following day.

It's vital I think that all young footballers learn to appreciate their standing in society. I know football is a sport, but there are an awful lot of people, both young and old who look to players to set an example. With youngsters always eager to copy their heroes, they should be given the right example and I'm afraid now and again football lets itself down by behaving badly. How can players or clubs complain about violence amongst fans, when you see players fighting on the pitch? Violence on the field is not a direct cause of hooliganism, but can act as a catalyst. Fortunately most footballers now realize the responsibility they have so let's hope the fans take note. Because football is played with passion in this country there are bound to be times when players get a little overheated or too excited, but we must all learn not to let things run away. I think one of the saddest things in football is to see youngsters copying some of the professionals by showing dissent and arguing with referees and linesmen. As a captain it falls on my shoulders to deal with referees more than most and although there are times when a particular decision can seem cruel there is a point to which you can go, if you think he's wrong, but after that you must respect his decision. That old word again . . . respect.

Invariably in football a well disciplined player is a good player and good behaviour has been the hallmark of nearly all of the great players in recent times. One chap who used to puzzle me was the Scottish International winger Willie Johnston, whom I played with at Albion. He was the classic example to all youngsters of how your game can be affected by getting into trouble on the field. Willie was a lovable man. He always had a joke to tell but could be very cutting with his remarks. He was a character; a man who livened up the dressing room. Willie off the field was a fairly even tempered man, but on it, there were occasions when he'd lose his head and by now he must hold the world record for being sent off! He was, in his day, a brilliantly talented player, but his discipline let him down and I'm convinced that had Willie been better behaved at times he would have written his name into the record books for far more illustrious reasons than being sent off. In the end Willie was a marked man. His opponents knew how to get him to lose his temper and referees would always watch someone like him much closer. As football faces a critical period it is so important the players respond to the challenge by setting an example not only for the supporters but for the youngsters who one day hope to take their places at Old Trafford, White Hart Lane or Anfield.

One of the secrets of football is never accept defeat . . . as that marvellous poem 'If' points out: 'If you think you are beaten, you are.'

## 16

# *A Memorable Season*

Wherever in the world football is played the name of Manchester United is known. It holds a special place in the hearts of millions. And mainly because on February 6 1958 a plane taking the United team home from a European Cup tie in Belgrade crashed on take-off at Munich airport. Twenty-one people, seven of them players were killed in the crash on that winter's day, and two others, including the legendary Duncan Edwards, died later in hospital. The effect on the club, Manchester and Britain was catastrophic. Never had so many talented sportsmen been killed. Apart from big Duncan, Roger Byrne, Eddie Coleman, David Pegg, Geoff Bent, Tommy Taylor, Mark Jones and Bill Whelan all died. Even to someone like me, who was only a baby at the time, the names still live on. You only have to look back in the old football annuals to read what great players they were. Nobody has allowed us to forget what happened on that day in Munich, and I hope they never will. The loss to football, and to Manchester United was immeasurable and so, when the New Year brought in 1983, and the twenty-fifth anniversary of the Munich disaster, it was time to look back and remember. One of the attractions of United is its tradition and every player who pulls on the red shirt knows instantly that he has a certain reputation to keep and live up to. A reputation of playing skilful and entertaining football. A reputation of making United one of the most successful clubs in the world.

The memory of those Manchester men who gave their

lives at Munich still helps to motivate the club. If not for that crash, they would have undoubtedly risen to become the most prolific side anyone has ever known. So, at United, there's a feeling we still owe it to the memory of the Busby Babes to keep the team battling for cups and major honours. And the twenty-fifth anniversary was a particularly poignant time at Old Trafford. Comparisons were drawn between the present side and that of the late fifties. I was even put alongside Duncan Edwards and Bobby Charlton as the whole club was awash with nostalgia.

Apart from the anniversary, the 1983 season was an important one for us because the honeymoon was over. Ron Atkinson had been there a year, so too had I and Frank Stapleton, the other big money signing from Arsenal, and you could sense a feeling amongst the supporters of expectancy. The money had been paid, they had patiently and loyally followed the team into third spot, and now they expected something more.

After Ray Wilkins was injured I was made captain and found myself with the unbeatable challenge of taking United to the top. The season started well. After four weeks we were at the top of the first division but the setback was that we were out of Europe, beaten by Valencia in the first round of the UEFA Cup. So, without that, we had to concentrate on the league and the Milk Cup. In the first division we were holding our own, but after a three week spell at the top, dropped back to fifth spot, as the mighty Liverpool began to force the pace.

In the Milk Cup we'd had a more uncomfortable ride than we'd bargained for. Bournemouth were our first opponents and we put them out with a 2-0 win at Old Trafford followed by a 2-2 draw down there on the south coast. Next came Bradford City. Over fifteen and a half thousand fans, their biggest crowd in years, packed into Valley Parade on a sharp November evening, and we were relieved to come away with a 0-0 draw. It had been a typical cup encounter. The third division men played as they'd never done before, running and chasing after the ball as though their lives depended on it. We were trying to take our time and be cool, but in those sorts of games, you end up reverting to the tactics of your opponents by hustling and bustling the match along. At Old Trafford, we found our feet and went marching on to the next round with a 4-1 win. We were lucky to get the home draw against Southampton, and although the Saints put up quite a fight, we eased our way through to the quarter finals with a 2-0 victory.

As Christmas came we were well on the way in the Milk Cup, second in the first division, and the FA Cup was also about to get underway. Ron Atkinson at last had his team playing well, and with his assistant Mick Brown was looking ahead to a rosy New Year. While Ron Atkinson blew the United trumpet, his worthy lieutenant Mick Brown got us knuckling down to prepare for the New Year. Mick was with Ron at Albion, and probably knows and understands me better than anyone in football. If ever anything goes wrong he can usually put his finger on the trouble in no time at all, and he has always been a tremendous source of good advice and encouragement.

We started 1983 well. We beat Villa 3-1 on New Year's Day and in the third round of the FA Cup knocked out West Ham in front of our own crowd. The Hammers are always a difficult team to beat, but an enjoyable one to play against because they like to come forward, and so you find yourself with more time and space. A 2-0 win in the third round gave us a match at Luton, but before that we had the next hurdle in the Milk Cup to overcome. We all knew how vital the next few weeks were going to be, and realized our season could be made or ruined here. United were still in the running for three competitions. Liverpool were ten points clear of us at the top of the first division, but there were still eighteen games to go. We'd made it to the quarter finals of the Milk Cup and had the advantage of a home tie against Nottingham Forest, and we were also well fancied in the FA Cup. There was even talk of the treble in Manchester, but I think all the players knew that was asking too much. We were happy, in good form and prepared to keep rolling along and taking each game in turn. Footballers are often ridiculed for their overuse of clichés. One that you hear every week on the radio or television or read in the papers happens when a player is asked about the big match at the week-end or the cup replay.

'Tell me,' says the interviewer, 'how important is this one?'

'Well,' says the player, 'it's a vital game, but we're just going to take it as it comes.'

Taking it as it comes might well be a well worn phrase, but it happens to be a footballer's philosophy. There's no good worrying about more than one match. So on Saturday if it's Liverpool in the league, then that's what you have to worry about. If you're down to play Spurs in the cup on Wednesday, then you start planning for that on Monday morning. Players don't often look further than the next match . . . it pays not to sometimes. As one of the old hands at United told me once, 'Don't start dreaming of Wembley until you're walking out there on Cup Final day.' But as we faced Nottingham Forest in the quarter final of the Milk Cup in January, there was, inevitably, Wembley talk in the air, mainly amongst the supporters. And some already booked their tickets after we crushed Brian Clough's team 4-0.

The following week it was the FA Cup, and at Luton we played soundly to earn a 2-0 victory, and a place in the fifth round. In the Milk Cup we were drawn against Arsenal in the two legged semi-final, while Liverpool played little Burnley in the other. We'd been hoping, of course, to catch Burnley and let Arsenal and Liverpool do battle, but in many respects it didn't really matter, because we would have to face one of them in the final if we got there. Arsenal though, were not having the best of seasons, and at Highbury in the first leg we caught them cold. This was the chance, Ron Atkinson said before the match, to really show what we were capable of. A good performance in London always seems to catch the headlines, and there was plenty to write about as we overcame the Gunners 4-2. That was on the Tuesday. On the Saturday we were at Derby for the fifth round of the FA Cup, with the second leg of the Arsenal game the following Wednesday at Old Trafford. We were playing so well, that apart from a daily workout to keep in trim, there wasn't much call for training, and the manager was more concerned to make sure we rested up well in between the matches.

The Derby cup tie on the Saturday was a hard one. Under their new manager Peter Taylor they were anxious to regain some of their past glory. Derby with Clough and Taylor in charge, had won the league championship in the seventies, but were now fighting to stay alive in the second division. We squeezed through, thanks to a Norman Whiteside goal near the end, and then everything was concentrated on Arsenal and the Milk Cup semi-final. With a 4-2 lead under our belts from the first match, the only major threat was complacency. Most of our supporters had taken it for granted we'd be at Wembley now, and Ron Atkinson made sure the same sort of feeling didn't get hold of us. The players naturally knew the dangers, and realized Arsenal were far from finished.

What should have been an enjoyable game, leading United to a Wembley final, turned into a nightmare for me. In the first half I went in to challenge for the ball and went over on my ankle. The pain was intense as my legs folded underneath me, and a cold tingling feeling crept through my body. I couldn't help but think back to those broken legs at West Bromwich, and wondered whether fate had struck me down again. It didn't feel broken, but when the United physio Jim McGregor knelt down by the side of me, I could tell he was having the same ghastly thoughts. The stretcher came on and I was whisked away to hospital. The sweat was pouring off me, and my mind raced away with worry. The sense of relief at hospital when I was told there was no break was overwhelming, but with the good news came the bad. There could be damage to the ankle ligaments, and it meant putting my leg in plaster. I was taken into the ward and kept in overnight. News of United's 2-1 victory arrived, and I didn't know whether to laugh or cry. I was overjoyed for the team and the supporters at reaching Wembley and the Milk Cup Final, but I knew my chances of being there with them were slim.

Some think I'm injury prone, and at times it looks that way, but my game is based on challenging for and winning the ball. You can't hold back in tackles because it's determination that wins in the end, and I don't go in to come out second! The injury news was a little brighter the next day; it might be nothing worse than a badly sprained ankle, but with the final only a month away, it was going to be a demanding four weeks. Having broken my leg three times, I knew the danger there was of coming back too soon, and my mind was torn in two. Half of me was saying, take your time and make sure you don't try anything too difficult until the ankle has healed and if it means missing the final hard luck. The other half was encouraging me to fight back, beat the injury and play at Wembley. As the weeks went by, everyone kept a close watch on my battle for fitness. Gradually the pain got less and when I returned to training the final was two weeks away. There was a chance I'd be able to lead United out against Liverpool, and Jim McGregor worked overtime on the treatment table. Not enough credit is given to football physios. They're always under pressure to get players ready in time, and yet know the consequences, if they gamble and send out a man who is not fully fit. Every day I was on the treatment table, and it's just as well that Jim is a lively chap with a good sense of humour, because just lying there as the machines purr away can be very frustrating.

In the meantime, United had beaten Everton in the quarter finals of the FA Cup, so when my prospects of making the Milk Cup Final against Liverpool started to dwindle, I could at least look forward with some hope to possibly an FA Cup Final. As we entered the run-in to the final I was still having intense treatment, but I knew in my own mind that I would not be fit in time. The club was buoyant with confidence, and for me life was difficult.

Fit or not, I was going to Wembley and was part of the squad, but there is no compensation for not playing. My heart was with them, but how I wished I could be playing. Another week and I would have made it, but I had to settle for a place on the bench on the big day. In the dressing room it was a peculiar feeling, not getting changed, and I felt a little detached as Ron Atkinson went through his team talk. The game itself was a disappointment for us. We could have won it so easily, but it was Liverpool who climbed the steps to get the trophy after winning 2-1 in extra time. They say it's worse losing a semi-final than a final, but I can tell you the feeling of disappointment in the United dresssing room was intense. The boss though, tried to pick us off the floor by telling us we'd be back in May for the FA Cup Final and after all, that was the one that mattered most of all. With Liverpool having taken the Milk Cup and built up a sixteen point lead at the top of the table, only the FA Cup was left. We were drawn against Arsenal at Villa Park in Birmingham, while the other semi-final was a battle of the underdogs. Relegation-threatened Brighton faced second division Sheffield Wednesday at Highbury. For us, the Arsenal semi-final was a mighty challenge. Driven on by the disappointment of losing to Liverpool at Wembley, we were determined to make up for it in the FA Cup. My ankle was mended and all of us relished the chance to get back to Wembley. Our games against Arsenal are always hard and toughly fought, and in the opening few minutes they gave us warning of what was to come. I was caught in at least two crunching tackles and looking around at the Arsenal team, I knew we had a fight on our hands. The Gunners took the lead through Tony Woodcock after thirty-five minutes, and at half-time there was just an air of tension in the United dressing room. Ron Atkinson paced up and down trying to settle us all down.

'We've got forty-five minutes to go out there and get to Wembley. Relax and play your football, and don't let them panic you.'

I knew that we needed a goal badly at the start of the second half. The longer Arsenal could hold on to that lead, the more powerful they'd become. Thankfully, after four minutes an opening came. I managed to shake off the Arsenal defence and cracked the ball past George Wood for the equalizer. That was the breakthrough we wanted, and I knew we would make it to Wembley again. With twenty minutes to go Norman Whiteside hit a beautiful winner and Arsenal were beaten. With Wembley and an FA Cup Final on the horizon, there was no way I was going to let this match out of our grip now, and what rejoicing there was when the whistle went . . . United 2 Arsenal 1 . . . Next stop Wembley Stadium and the Cup Final against Brighton and Hove Albion. Before the final, of course, we had our own league games, and I remembered offering up a prayer in the Villa Park dressing room, not to get injured again this time.

The Milk Cup Final earlier in the season, had caused an awful lot of interest in Manchester, but there's nothing to beat the FA Cup. It's still the one trophy that every player dreams of winning, let's face it Cup Final day at Wembley in May, is still the showpiece of English football.

With the Cup Final came an unbelievable amount of work and pressure. Suddenly the phone started to ring, and of course, everyone wanted a ticket for the big day. The Robson family was coming down from Chester-le-Street for the match and Denise's relations wanted to be there as well. There were friends to sort out, and at one stage, I reckoned I could have got rid of another ten thousand tickets or so. There were numerous commercial activities tied in with sponsors to carry out, and everyone wanted to either take a picture of the team or talk to you. As the captain, I was one of the prime targets, and I wondered at one stage whether I was going to have a voice left for the big day.

The week of the final was absolute murder. We travelled to London in preparation, but once there, hardly had any time to ourselves. Television, radio and newspapers were all knocking on our doors, and as the match got nearer, so the demand increased for interviews.

United were red hot favourites naturally enough, which did not worry us too much because we were confident of beating Brighton. But we also knew that at Wembley all teams are equal and Brighton had beaten Liverpool at Anfield on their way to the final. That in itself was an achievement deserving a trophy. To be honest, I didn't enjoy the Saturday as much as I thought I would because our preparations were not natural. We'd been living under the glare of publicity all week, and even on the Saturday there was no let up. At ten o'clock in the morning there was a knock on my bedroom door at the hotel where we were staying and on the doorstep was a television camera crew who wanted to have one last interview with me. So, while I had a morning shave in the mirror, they asked me about the final, but I appreciate that Cup Final day is a football ritual so didn't mind too much. People like to watch their teams making their way down Wembley Way, as thousands of supporters head for the stadium. To be honest, I think we're in danger of overdoing it at times, because all the elaborate preparations and publicity got to United and affected our performance. On the way to the stadium, we again had a television crew aboard the coach, and as you stepped on to the pitch for the first time there were reporters and cameramen there to ask you, for the hundredth time, what your feelings were. In short, we never had time to settle or feel ourselves, and the only privacy we had was in the dressing room just before the game. When the door was finally shut, with only half an hour to go, we could at last gather our thoughts and make the final plans and preparations.

Backstage at Wembley is totally different from any

other football ground I know. The dressing rooms have more a feeling of an old station waiting room, while outside, officials are pacing up and down looking at their watches every two seconds or so. Cup Final day is run to military precision. You have to be in the tunnel by a certain time, and you're told which side to stand. You walk out to a signal, and have something like two minutes to make it to the area in front of the Royal Box for the presentations.

When the knock on the door came for us to take our places, the Cup Final anthem 'Abide with Me' was just fading in the distance. I was sad in a way to have missed that, because that hymn always stirs me inside, and I love to hear the Wembley crowd singing it. Sadly, it tends to get drowned by the chants of the younger supporters these days, but I wish they'd join in more with the sense of the occasion. We lined up alongside Brighton in the tunnel, and exchanged nods and hellos before the order came to walk out. It was a walk I'd made a thousand times before in my dreams. A wall of sound hit us emerging into the sun; everywhere people were on their feet, waving banners and colours. It must be one of the most satisfying and enjoyable moments in any footballer's career. I'd made the walk with England and led them out at Wembley before now, but Cup Final day was something special. Here we were on one of Britain's great sporting days, lapping it all up. For those two minutes as we made our way out, I totally forgot about the game, and drank it all in. We lined up for the presentation, and it was my job to take the Duke of Kent, the principal guest, down the line of players. He wished us all well, and there was a kind word of encouragement from the FA Chairman Bert Millichip, who'd been in charge at West Bromwich Albion.

For me, the Final was a little disappointing. I didn't play as well as I should have done, and United were never at their best. I sensed something was wrong, when Brighton took the lead early on. Second half goals from Frank Stapleton and Ray Wilkins took us into the lead, and, as Ron Atkinson signalled five minutes to go from the bench, I thought we were going to make it. But Cup Finals have a habit of saving the exciting bits to the last, and with just four minutes to go, Stevens equalized, and with only seconds left Brighton missed the chance of the match. Smith was clear and his shot was saved by Gary Bailey, when it would have been an awful lot easier to score. So, when the whistle went after extra time, there was a peculiar feeling of relief and yet disappointment. We could have won, although we hadn't played as well as we were capable of. On the other hand, Brighton could have snatched it at the death. After climbing the steps to shake hands with the guests in the Royal Box, we went on a lap of honour, but a final without a winner is an empty one, and as we waved to the crowd, my thoughts were already moving ahead to Thursday night and the replay.

The following day we had an even stranger job. It's always been common practice for the cup winners to parade the trophy through the streets of their town the next day, and Manchester had arranged an open top bus for us, through the middle of the city. It had to be done on the Sunday, because for one reason or another, no other date was convenient. So we all piled on to this open top bus and made our way through the streets for a reception at the Town Hall. Although there was no trophy to show off, the fans still came in their thousands to cheer us on.

After a day at home, it was back down to London to prepare for the replay, and this time we were much more settled and confident. On the Wednesday I did a couple of interviews for television, and that was that. On the day of the match we were left alone to gather our thoughts and prepare in private. There were no television crews or cameramen this time as we left the hotel and made our way to the stadium. It was more like a normal match day, and all the players appreciated it. We knew that, if we settled and played our normal game we could sweep Brighton aside. They were a plucky team, and could play given the chance, but it was up to us to take the Cup. Without all the trappings of the Saturday, we felt at home in the replay, and after twenty-four minutes took the lead. Albiston started the move and then I picked up a cross from young Alan Davies and drove it into the Brighton net. What elation; a Wembley goal! Four minutes later Norman Whiteside got the second, and then just before half-time I got another to make it 3-0. We knew then that we'd done it. All we had to do was keep our heads, Brighton were beaten.

In the second half we controlled the game and made it four when Stevens pulled me back as I strode towards goal and we were awarded a penalty. One or two of the lads suggested I take it so I could get a hat trick, but Arnie Muhren was penalty taker in Steve Coppell's absence, and there seemed no reason to change. Arnold made no mistake and it was time to celebrate. United had won the cup 4-0.

We hugged and congratulated each other, and then made for the thirty-nine steps and glittering FA Cup. I started off taking the steps two at a time, but then remembered something I'd heard other players say about Wembley. They said they'd rushed the end too much and not been able to enjoy it as they should. So, I slowed down, and carefully made my way to the top savouring the cheers and congratulations. On the way up, we were slapped on the back by the overjoyed United fans, and as women leaned over to kiss us, others tried to tie scarves round our necks. At the top of the steps I was aware of somebody patting me on the head, but by then, all I could see was the FA Cup with its red and white ribbons adorning the handles. The United directors were there, and so too was Sir Matt. It was his birthday, and what better present could the lads have given him. It was twenty-five years since his team of young dazzlers had been cruelly pulled apart by that plane crash, and by some divine chance, all those years later the name of Manchester United was on the lips once more, as winners of one of football's most prestigious trophies, the FA Cup. Princess Michael was the guest of honour for the replay, and after shaking hands, I lifted the cup and proudly pushed it in the air. Wembley was alight. The glare of the floodlights and the flash bulbs of the cameras bounced off the silver trophy. United had done it and I had fulfilled a lifelong dream. That night we celebrated, and it wasn't until I got home and watched the game on video, that I realized I'd committed a terrible crime. When I was at the top of the steps at the Royal Box I can remember somebody patting me on the head, but I didn't realize I was wearing a supporter's silk cap. So when I went to shake hands with the Princess and lift the cup, there I was wearing this hat. I felt ashamed because, had I realized I was wearing the hat, I would have taken it off before meeting the Princess. Denise commented about it too, and it seemed bad mannered not to take my hat off when meeting royalty. I thought for a long time about writing to Princess Michael to apologize for my slip, but if I'm ever lucky enough to meet her again, will make my apologies.

A Wembley final was a fitting farewell to the season, and within a few months we were back there beating

Liverpool in the annual clash of the champions, The Charity Shield.

From my first days as a footballer I'd always wanted to play at Wembley, and looking back, I appreciate how lucky I've been. But what's more important is the re-emergence of Manchester United.

Getting to the top in football is a long climb, but staying there is an even greater feat. Over the years I've faced many different challenges. First there was my weight problem at Albion, then the broken legs. After that came the record-breaking transfer, the World Cup in Spain followed by the chance to captain both my club and country.

What more could I ask for from football? Two challenges are left . . . to lead England to victory in the 1986 World Cup, and to establish Manchester United once and for all as the greatest club side the world has ever known.

# 17
## *To the Future*

A bitterly cold night in the Grand Duchy of Luxembourg was perhaps one of my saddest in football. As the England team sat in the dressing room waiting for the kick-off the news came that Denmark had beaten Greece which meant there was no place for us in the European Championships. I can never remember a dressing room being so low. The news killed us all, and for twenty minutes or so nobody said a word. All you could hear was the clatter of boots on the floor as the players went through their usual rituals of getting ready. Even manager Bobby Robson sat silently as he and all the rest of us sat and reflected on our failure. When we'd first arrived at the stadium we'd been lifted by news that Denmark were losing, but unhappily someone had got the wrong end of the stick and the England team had to sit and face the future.

In that long silent pause before running out to face Luxembourg I imagine each and every player searched his conscience to find out where we had failed. The one big mistake, of course, was losing to Denmark at Wembley earlier on, but apart from that we hadn't been that far away. Even though the Danes were a more organized and skilled side than most would give them credit for, it was now our fault that England would not be going to join the rest of the top nations for the championship. England players have been accused of lacking pride or passion when playing for their country, but I think anyone who'd walked into that dressing room in Luxembourg would have realized where our hearts were. Success meant everything to the squad and to be discarded on the scrapheap was perhaps the worst feeling of all. Injuries at crucial times had disrupted our preparation but we all knew it should have been England and not Denmark en route to France. I've never seen so many long faces in a dressing room before a match. If you'd have walked in you would have thought we'd just come off after a five nil defeat rather than be preparing to start. Our victory against Luxembourg at least showed some of the fighting spirit and pride England still had and I'm sure each and every player vowed there and then that next time we'd be at the front of the queue.

The next time, of course, is Mexico and the 1986 World Cup Finals. England have been waiting too long for success and the players are now hungrier than ever. Having let everyone down in the past all we can do is make amends and I know we have the ability, not only to make Mexico, but also to win the cup again after a break of twenty years. England to me has always been the home of football and it's wrong we should struggle to find success when the country possesses so many talented players. I suppose every England captain or manager makes brave predictions about the future, but we have at last good reason for being confident.

In manager Bobby Robson, we have a man who has now gained a few years of valuable experience at full international level to complement those with his former club Ipswich Town. No manager can expect to leave the first division arena and find instant success on the international field. The jobs are poles apart. As a club manager you're busy from day to day with players and all the other people that make up a club. With England, there is perhaps more time to consider and plan things but you have to be prepared for some intensive training on the few occasions the players all get together.

Bobby Robson has the backing of all the England players and we are confident that he is the right man to take us to the next World Cup. Over the past two years he has been forced to experiment with younger players and inexperienced ones but now the squad is taking shape and it is young enough and good enough to last to Mexico. I think the secret for England now is to keep a settled side, so that when the World Cup comes around we have a well balanced, organized and highly experienced squad. The years of transition are almost over and Bobby Robson has just about got it right. There are bound to be one or two changes on the way but if most of the present team can stay together we have, I believe, a great chance. In defence, players such as Mike Duxbury, Terry Butcher and Kenny Sansom are getting better with every game. Mike has matured well at Old Trafford and his natural speed and ability should serve England well. The form of Terry Butcher though, is perhaps most important in the defence because a strong and commanding centre-half can make all the difference. Terry has been a promising player for years but now he is hardening into a first class international. So much depends on him. His power in the air and presence at the heart of the defence is vital. When he first played for England Terry naturally suffered from nerves and inexperience. He has come through that now and when the next World Cup arrives will have matured, I think, into one of England's finest central defenders.

In midfield we have plenty of talented players, but what's more important is that we are beginning to play to each other's strengths more and more. Switching from club to international football is difficult when you're thrown in with men you've never played alongside before.

Look how long it takes a player to really settle in to a new team in the first division – perhaps a season. With Ray Wilkins, Sammy Lee, Glen Hoddle, and Gary Mabbutt we are building a skilful engine room to run the side and all of us aim to be on the plane for Mexico in two years' time. Even the goals are beginning to come and the player I should like to see wearing the number nine shirt for England in the World Cup is Cyrille Regis of West Bromwich Albion. Cyrille has been unlucky with injury at the start of his England career but I believe he is just the right man for the job. To me, Regis is how a perfect centre-forward would come off any designer's drawing board. Good in the air, clever on the ground and with a turn of speed which would test any defender, Cyrille has all the ingredients, and what's more given the right service and with back up can produce goals galore. There are several strikers in the queue for England and many of them are worth a place, but I would like to see Cyrille Regis given a chance to show Bobby Robson what he can do.

One of the biggest ambitions I have now in football is to lead England to a World Cup win. It's something I long to do and I believe another great national team is emerging in this country. Given good fortune and the chance to work together more often I am convinced we will be there this time. A footballer's career is like a rolling stone travelling down a slope – it seems to build up speed and get faster all the time. One minute you're just making your debut and the next you are being talked of as an old hand. My football life seems to have raced past, but at the age of twenty-seven there's still a lot I want to do. Winning the FA Cup with United was one of my first ambitions and next on the list must be the league championship. The FA Cup has that magical glory, but to a footballer the real proof of success is winning the championship. Over the past few seasons we have been desperately close, but now at last at Old Trafford we have, I think, the strongest all round team in the country. Ron Atkinson, with the backing of the board has done a first class job since he's been there. He has consistently worked hard to bring a talented squad together, and his search for the best has been relentless.

You only have to look at Liverpool to find the recipe for success. Over the last twenty years they have never stopped building so that when a player is injured or loses form there is another, equally as good, to take his place. Now United are on the same trail. Ron Atkinson has not just built an eleven man team but a twenty man squad. The days when a football club relied on eleven men and a substitute are long gone. In a world as competitive as the first division you need at least sixteen or seventeen good players to do well. With United adopting such a policy life at Old Trafford is exciting. It is so encouraging to belong to a team and play for a manager where everyone is actively chasing the same dreams as yourself. A strong squad means competition for places in the team and that too is a good thing. So many clubs build a side and then sit back and enjoy a good run of three or four seasons. Suddenly one or two players lose form and the side is struggling with nobody at the back to replace them. At Old Trafford we all know that only the best is good enough. It's not a case of anxiously looking over your shoulder, but I know if I went through a lean patch and lost my form, there would be someone pressing to take my place. I've got no plans to vacate that number seven shirt yet though because the Manchester United crusade is only just beginning.

Apart from league championships I would also like to

see us emulate the great teams of Sir Matt Busby and conquer Europe again . . . the UEFA Cup, Cup Winner's Cup and Champion's Cup, what a treble that would be.

Rumours about Italian clubs such as AC Milan paying out between three or four million pounds for me persist, but I can tell them now they are wasting their time. My allegiance is to Manchester United. Perhaps in a few years time, when my contract at Old Trafford ends, I would consider going abroad, either to Europe or America to play. It's something I wouldn't mind trying, but any move, to Italy or anywhere else is a long way in the future.

To me the English first division is still the best in the world. Playing for Manchester United and belonging to the Old Trafford tradition is the fulfilment of a dream. United, I believe is still the most powerful name in club football anywhere in the world. They will always be the best supported team in this country and what more could a footballer ask for than to be captain of Manchester and England?

# 18

## *Curtain Call*

Save the best until last is a rule that most top entertainers like to stick to; hopefully, when the curtain finally falls, the audience will be left cheering and wanting more. Most footballers I know are the same. They are entertainers, and there's nothing they like more than leaving the fans applauding their success.

It doesn't always work out that way of course, as we discovered at Old Trafford last season. Having won the FA Cup at Wembley and come close in the Championship, we all hoped that the 83–84 season would see us establishing ourselves even more.

What better start could we have had than the Charity Shield match at Wembley in August, where as FA Cup winners we faced Liverpool, the League Champions? It was the 75th Charity Shield game and it turned out to be quite a landmark for United as well. A 2-0 win over Liverpool is always something to be savoured, and with both goals falling my way at Wembley, you could not blame us for being confident about the season ahead. A victory over the Liverpool machine is worth two or three against other sides, and I honestly thought as we prepared for the months ahead that United had the strength and style to beat the Anfield men to the League Championship. On the opening day, just under 50,000 were at Old Trafford, and a 3-1 win over Queens Park Rangers was a good result to start with. Two days later, though, with 43,000 in the ground, we lost to Nottingham Forest, more a disappointment than a setback.

The first few weeks of a football season can sometimes be the worst. You often get teams that are out of the blocks like sprinters and amaze everyone, including themselves quite often, by pulling away to the top of the first division. Then there are the fancied sides that perhaps have a slow and hesitant start to the season. If that happens the alarm bells start ringing and the pressure is on. Fortunately, after that defeat at home to Forest, we picked ourselves up and knocked off three straight wins over Stoke, Arsenal and Luton. A slight stutter saw us go down 3–0 at Southampton but on the last Saturday in September we were up against our arch-enemy Liverpool again.

The biggest league crowd of the season (56,121) crammed into Old Trafford, and a second-half goal from Frank Stapleton gave us our second victory over Liverpool in five weeks. For most United fans the League Championship was over there and then. They were convinced that the win over Liverpool was the sign they had been waiting for and that it was going to be United's year.

I must admit I felt confident as well. The team was beginning to play well, and in October we pushed our way to the top for the first time. Liverpool, as always though, were breathing down our necks, and they took over as league leaders at the start of November after a win in the derby game against Everton, and believe it or not, apart from one week in March, they stayed there with us chasing them. When United went top in the middle of March our Championship hopes were refuelled, and with our performances in the European Cup Winner's Cup against Barcelona we were on our way.

The second leg of the Cup Winner's Cup quarter-final against the Spanish side was one of the best matches I've ever played in. The setting could not have been better.

Having lost the first leg over in Spain 2–0 it needed a mighty effort from us to save the tie. Old Trafford was fuller than I've ever seen it, and with over 58,000 voices cheering us on it felt as though we were a goal up before we even kicked off.

Although many wrote us off before the game, thinking that it was impossible to give a team such as Barcelona with Maradona a two-goal start, we were all convinced that we could do it. The result over in Spain had been such a disappointment to us that we were determined to fight back and show that Manchester United were still one of Europe's top sides. In a game of passion and high drama we squeezed home with a 3–0 win on a memorable night that I'm sure the United fans, and come to that the players as well, will not forget.

Sadly, injury hit then, and I missed the semi-final against Juventus. After a 1–1 draw at Old Trafford we went down 2–1 over in Italy, and that was one of the cups out of our grasp.

The two English cups, the FA and the Milk Cup, were also out of reach by then, with third-division teams knocking us out of both. In the Milk Cup it was Oxford United – the high riding cavaliers re-born under the chairmanship of Robert Maxwell and the managership of Jim Smith. It took three long, hard games to sort it out, with Oxford finally putting us out in the second replay at the Manor Ground. For United it was a blow to lose, and embarrassing to fall to a club from the lower divisions, though Oxford were by no means an average third-division side – with players like Bobby McDonald, Neil Whatmore and Mick Vinter in the team, they were a skilled and experienced outfit. They proved as much by winning the third-division Championship and in many respects I didn't mind being beaten by a team of such quality.

It was a different story, though, in the FA Cup. The third round draw took us for a day at the seaside and a game against Bournemouth. For them, of course, it was the big match of the season. What a bonus for the third division men, a home draw against the FA Cup holders Manchester United! When you are drawn against such sides in the cup competitions there is always a worry, because you don't know much about them and they are hard to predict. They always raise their game for the Manchester Uniteds of the world, and we have to try and keep our heads and rely on our experience and skills to get us through.

This time though, it didn't quite go to plan, and Bournemouth hit the headlines with a 2–0 win. It was of course the shock result of the day, and while the seaside town celebrated their most famous win in years, we were left humiliated and hurt.

The defeat was painful. Having won at Wembley the season before it was a shattering blow to go out in the third round to a third-division team. The papers and the television pundits made a meal of it. Bournemouth were the heroes that weekend, and although we were made to suffer it was a result that proved once again the pulling power of the FA Cup. When teams like Bournemouth can play against, and beat, first division teams such as United, it provides great excitement for the competition, but losing out as we did is not an experience I would like to have too often.

So, with both the FA Cup and the Milk Cup lost, and later of course the Cup Winner's Cup gone, it was all down to the league. With nine matches to go, only two points separated us from Liverpool, who were on top. Nottingham Forest were seven points behind us, with West Ham and Southampton two behind them. It looked really like a straight fight between United and Liverpool.

We matched them stride for stride then. While we beat Birmingham City, they put six past West Ham. The following week they lost at Stoke, but we went down as well at Notts County. Looking back that was a real blow, because a victory at Meadow Lane would have taken us to the top, and we would have set the pace from there on in.

In the next four matches we drew three and won one – and incredibly Liverpool did exactly the same. Three games to go and still there were just two points in it, although Queens Park Rangers and Southampton were both coming with late finishes. Our last three games were Ipswich at home followed by Spurs and Forest away, while Liverpool faced an easier finish on paper with Coventry, Notts County and Norwich City.

While we stumbled to defeat against Ipswich at Old Trafford, Liverpool cracked five past Coventry City, with Ian Rush getting four of them. Two matches to go and Liverpool were now five points clear. The Championship was clearly slipping away from us, and when we drew at Spurs and they were held at Notts County, the chase for United was over. But worse was still to come. Liverpool took the title for the third year running. United, for so long the only other contenders, lost at Forest in the last game and were overtaken by both them and Southampton and left in fourth position.

After so many high spots it was bitterly disappointing to finish the season without a trophy, and in some respects I take the blame for United's failure. Towards the end of the season rumours and speculation about my future with the club were rife. Money was no object to some of the Italian clubs who were reported to be ready with fabulous offers and contracts. Although the transfer talk niggled me a bit, it proved unsettling for the club, I think. On a personal level I was determined to show my loyalty to

United, but rumours that the club could be losing not only its captain but another precious player, Ray Wilkins, didn't do much for team confidence.

It all came at a critical time, as well. Just when United should have been pulling everything out for a whirlwind finish to the season, the club was riddled with doubt about the future. Although Ron Atkinson was determined not to let me go, there was no stopping the talk from Europe, and I'm sure it was one of the reasons behind our slump at the end of the season.

The loss of Ray Wilkins to Italy was a blow of course, but in Gordon Strachan and Jasper Olsen United have two world-class players who will grow stronger as they get to know United. I was sad to see Ray go because he had always been a close friend and a great man to have alongside you. But hopefully we will be able to keep our partnership going with England, and march towards the World Cup.

As for me, well I'm glad that the transfer talk has blown over. I'm happy and settled at Old Trafford and enjoy my family life here in England. Money can never buy happiness and I would be quite content to see my days out with Manchester United. And I hope that sooner or later United will take a few curtain calls as we save the best until last . .

# Index